The SUPRA-NATURAL

hope the story of Christ in you

Paul & Coroline Holbrook

CHRISTEN FORSTER

C000165079

RIVER

PUBLISHING

River Publishing & Media Ltd
Barham Court
Teston
Maidstone
Kent
ME18 5BZ
United Kingdom

info@river-publishing.co.uk

All Scripture quotations are based on the author's own translation.

ISBN 978-1-908393-35-7

Printed in the United Kingdom
Cover design by www.SpiffingCovers.com

CONTENTS

DEDICATION

For my parents, Roger and Faith Forster:
You showed me Jesus in words, in actions and with power, and
you walked me through so many of these stories.

ACKNOWLEDGEMENTS

First, a big "thank you" to all those friends who have walked with me through a tough season. Your encouragement and support have meant I've finished what I started. More specifically, I want to thank Ann and Alistair for pushing me to take time out to write, and I want to thank Darrell Cocup and Andrew McNeil for their help critiquing the text at various stages of development.

Finally, I want to thank my family – my wife, Judith, and three children, Joel, Kezia and Olivia – who carry the cost of my physical and mental absences when I get into writing mode.

WHAT OTHERS ARE SAYING ABOUT THE SUPRA-NATURAL HOPE

"Christen Forster does an outstanding job of explaining the difference between our identity and our calling; between God's plan for our life and our part in that plan. He provides us with understanding and insight on how our daily journey is part of fulfilling His plan for our life. The stories, examples and scriptures presented are of great encouragement and produce excitement in my heart. I strongly encourage everyone to read *The Supra-Natural Hope!*"

Dr. Che' Ahn
Senior Pastor, HRock Church, Pasadena, CA
President, Harvest International Ministry
International Chancellor, Wagner Leadership Institute

"God made us in His image. The problem is, from the moment we're conceived the world conspires to separate us from that image. We're unwanted, abused, unloved, lonely, ignored, bullied, told we're stupid, that we'll never make anything of our lives ... things that wound us and plant lies about ourselves. We become people that God never intended us to be. Then a book like this comes along and the true nature and depth of God's love for us begins to be revealed. As you read, your spirit will resonate with Christen's teaching on identity; with how we've allowed God's gift of our unique identity to be stolen. But you will also learn how to walk in new freedom once again. I love this book, written from the heart for your heart."

Darrell Cocup
South West Regional Facilitator, Bethel Sozo UK

"Do you ever wonder where those inner desires have come from? We all have hopes, dreams and aspirations within our hearts.

Some are like germinating, God-given seeds found in Christ which, when encouraged to sprout and flourish, bring joyful fulfilment to our souls. Others are weeds that can only bring frustration and resentment. Christen's excellent book will help you discern the difference between the two by discovering in Christ the real 'you' and the dreams your Father has for you. Paradoxically, pausing to read this book will provide a fillip to the momentum of the Father's yearnings for you."

Dave Emmett
Principal, United School of Ministry, Manchester

"Undeniably doctrinally detailed – as you would expect from Christen Forster! But also abundantly practical – and an essential guide for any Christian to discover, plan a course towards and realise their dream – that for which God has purposed, made and equipped them."

Bill Partington
Head of Strategic Ministry Relations, UCB

"Christen Forster understands what I believe is the key issue facing the Church today – that is the mobilising of every Christian to be missional. Christian leaders will not change the nation, but the body of Christ can. This book empowers people to find out who they really are. It empowers them with a new hope about their identity and their calling; it is therefore significant and important for today."

Laurence Singlehurst
Director, Cell UK

"God dreams. Being created in His image, we also dream. So what happens when our dreams and His dreams converge? Power comes, things happen, and God is glorified in our midst. Christen Forster unfolds a vast resource of biblical references and practical testimony to show there's a big difference between being in church and being in Christ. This is an important book for understanding our identity. Not least because, if we know who we are in Christ and who Christ is in us, our identity will command our destiny. Illustrating how the Holy Spirit empowers and guides us to go beyond the limits of our self, our imaginations, and the world we are presented with, we come to understand our place in the story of God. This rollercoaster ride through the Kingdom of God is not only exciting stuff, it's the only show in town."

Dr David Landrum
Director of Advocacy, Evangelical Alliance

"Christen Forster thinks outside the box, so be prepared to be challenged and inspired by his latest book. He has seen major miracles in his personal life and ministry, but he has also experienced serious disappointments too. With this background and his unique approach to explaining biblical truth, he is well equipped to write on the subject of the hope of our calling in Christ. Christen picks up on two essentials for anyone longing to be fulfilled in their Christian life and journey: *identity* and *calling*. If we don't understand who we are in Christ we will never achieve our God-given destiny. Identity precedes function! This book will undoubtedly point you in the right direction and give you faith and courage to fulfil your destiny in Jesus."

John Noble
Pioneer of the New Church Movement in the UK

"Christen's latest book will encourage those on a journey of discovery into their Heavenly Father's wonderful and unique plan for their lives. We believe it will help them to be confident carriers of His Presence and His Hope wherever they might be."

Hugh and Ginny Cryer
Culture Changers, www.culture-changers.org

"In *Supranatural Hope*, Christen Foster challenges the reader to excavate their true God-dreams. The hope of your calling is understood only after cementing the profoundness of your true identity: 'child of God'. From this free-from-striving place of rest, Christen helps you prayerfully walk through practical insights from the Word with fresh Holy Spirit applications. You will find yourself dreaming the dreams of God and filled with a holy sense of opportunity and adventure once again. This is a must read!"

Georgian Banov

President and Co-Founder of Global Celebration and General Director of The Bulgarian Bible Project

"Christen is an anointed teacher who sets out the fundamental architecture of how you can live with an open heaven reality. In this book, through testimony and fresh biblical insight, you will be able to activate the Glory of God already inside you (Colossians 1:27). For this mystery be revealed to the world it needs sons and daughters of the King to rise up. I recommend this book if you want to live a life of knowing who you are, what you carry and how to release His glory to impact the world around you every day."

Andrew Chapman

Founder & CEO, London School of Supernatural Ministry

FOREWORD

There are very few books on Identity and Significance that call one into life, freedom and opportunity. More often, the recommendations turn out to be striving and "self-help", and only cause us to ultimately spiral down again.

In the *The Supra-Natural Hope* Christen Forster gives several keys, helping us to both rest and excel as we find our way through life's difficult challenges, both within and without. This transparent and well-written work cannot but help you take huge steps upward and onward to greater comprehension of identity, purpose and hope.

John Arnott
Catch the Fire Ministries, Toronto

INTRODUCTION

A Parable About Talents

On April 11th 2009, a middle-aged lady from West Lothian in Scotland went through a life-defining moment live on TV. I remember watching it happen.

Susan Boyle, a socially clumsy, somewhat eccentric 48 year-old with learning difficulties shambled onto the stage of "Britain's Got Talent". The nation sniggered when she said that she wanted, "to be as successful as Elaine Page." But then she opened her mouth and sang:

"I dreamed a dream in time gone by, when hope was high and life worth living…"[1]

Within ten days, clips of her audition had been watched over 100 million times on the Internet.

Her first album became the UK's biggest selling debut album ever and then, in 2012, Elaine Page actually played Susan Boyle on stage in a musical based on her life story.

Susan was clearly made to sing. She had tried to be a professional singer for a long time, but prejudice and her own fear had prevented her from stepping into her dream. But they hadn't stopped her singing. Susan was a singer whether the world recognised it or not.

"I dreamed a dream" has become a classic television moment, but I have a confession to make!

I was actually watching the show for the opposite phenomena: you know, those auditions where someone sings horribly off-key and out of rhythm and then refuses to believe that they don't have what it takes to make it to the next round, let alone to win the competition. I find these moments addictively painful to watch; conflicted by an urge to laugh and compassion for a soul so desperately self-deceived.

Like Susan, all these contestants have a dream too. But how can they be so wrong in their conception of who they are?

The answer is simple, yet profoundly important. If we don't understand the answer deeply it's highly unlikely we'll walk according to the plan, calling and identity the Father has for us.

It is primarily our emotional shape which drives us to act, not our knowledge, understanding and logic. We will do whatever we need to do to feel "worth it."

Ultimately, we draw our sense of worth from each other. Celebrities draw a little bit from a lot of people; a parent may draw a lot from a few children; an employer draws some from his employees; a businesswoman from her customers and so on. Each learns to do the things that will draw value from their audience whether that audience is their friends, their family, their work mates or the masses.

The need to feel "worth it" creates the steady supply of willing contestants ready to answer the call of the TV talent shows. Many are happy to jump at the chance of being one of the few chosen by the nation. Most, of course, fall into the reality gap between who they are and who they want to be.

Those willing to go on TV to showcase talents they don't have are just the tip of the iceberg. Whether in front of millions or in the quiet of our own hearts, for the majority it seems that life's adventure ends like the last line of Susan's song:

"So different now from what it seemed, now life has killed the dream I dreamed."

Dreams are the ideas our imagination clothes our deepest hopes and desires in. Dreams give shape to those elusive motivations that compel us onward and upward. We are supposed to have dreams. They can unlock life, but they are also a risky business and can lead to disappointment.

"A hope deferred makes the heart sick, but a desire that arrives is a tree of life." (Proverbs 13:12)

It's a vicious circle. We have warped emotional needs so we aim for achievements that aren't "us", but that we think will make us feel good. When we fail we are disappointed and create an even bigger need.

Television tends to magnify people's flaws so that they become unmissable. But most of us live with some degree of misshapen identity. We build up images of ourselves – who we are and who we will one day become – images that comfort us with the hope of future glory. But it is the kind of glory that comes from being on top of the pile or at the centre of attention, rather than the glory which Jesus promises us (John 17:22).

It's an uncomfortable truth, one that we might deny even to ourselves, but most of us feel a sense of worth if we are ahead of our friends in something they care about. Most of us have something we are relatively good at, so we search out peers who will value us for our talents.

If that's not enough we might pursue an "alternative lifestyle", because "being different" is a safer and kinder alternative to "being better". There may be no one below you, but there is no one above you either. You can be top of your pile of one and there's nothing like eccentricity to get you noticed.

Actually, there is nothing wrong with drawing value from others through our gifts and abilities, nor from a sense of our uniqueness. But the value we draw from these sources should be like a second income: an income that enables all sorts of treats and pleasures in life, but it is not the main resource from which we live day by day. We need to draw our value from God or we will end up sucking up more from others than they can safely give us.

But now here is the good news: there is an alternative. Father God has a good plan for your life, one that will confirm in you the value He's placed on you. So He calls you, not because He needs servants to do things for Him, but because He has sons and daughters who He wants to see reach their potential. The discovery of who you were made to be is an adventure to be lived. It may not get played out on the small screen before an audience of millions, nor get made into a stage play with Elaine Page playing your part. But your story does have an audience in God: Father, Son and Holy Spirit and a whole host of witnesses who have a stake in your story too, and they're all cheering you on.

Together we're going to try to discover the story already being written in you and see how it might grow going forward. So if you're sitting comfortably, we can begin.

Endnotes
1. "I dreamed a dream" from the musical "Les Miserables".

CHAPTER 1

THE HOPE OF HIS CALLING

"...that the eyes of your heart may be enlightened, that you may know what is *the hope of His calling*, and what is the rich value of the glory of His inheritance in the saints." (Ephesians 1:18)

This is a book about your calling!

If you walk in your calling, you will "bear... fruit that remains" (John 15:16) and leave an echo in eternity.[2]

To have a calling means more than just having a job to do. It points to a hope beyond the tasks, to your unique inheritance in Jesus. Your calling is the means by which Father releases the rich value of the glory in you.

So this is a book about your value too!

I have a twenty-pound note in my pocket. Like all British bank notes it carries an image of the Queen and it also has a band of sterling silver running through it. Without these two hallmarks a bank note is just a piece of paper.

Everybody carries God's image, it's how we are made (Genesis 1:27), and we have a silver band running through us too. It's the splash of His glory that make us what we are, the interface between earth and heaven.

"The Lord God formed man from the dust of the ground, and breathed into his nostrils *the breath of life*; and man became a living soul." (Genesis 2:7)[3]

The Hebrew word translated here as "breath", "neshemah", is a "gust of wind", a "pant of breath" or a "wisp of the Spirit", and the Spirit is "the Spirit of Glory and of God" (1 Peter 4:14). So we all have a splash of the Spirit of Glory in us, a bit like the strip of silver in a bank note and, by strange but useful coincidence, this deposit of the Spirit of Glory in our dust-formed bodies is likened to a silver band in Ecclesiastes.

"Before the silver band is broken, or the golden bowl is crushed... when the dust returns to the earth as it was, and the spirit returns to God who gave it." (Ecclesiastes 12:6-7)

God has put the hallmarks of heavenly value in us. On earth we are the currency that gives everything else its value.

Calling doesn't give us value, calling makes the most of the value in us.

Our calling exists within God's plan for us. This plan has several stages. Sometimes the stages overlap and, at other times, there is a clear break between them. As a result the details of our calling can seem to change as Jesus leads us from season to season. But there is a consistent hope in the unfolding call. It is the version of each of us that heaven has seen from the beginning.

This is a book about your life story, from cradle to eternity!

"For you formed my innermost being. You wove me together in my mother's womb. I will give thanks to you for I am awesomely and wonderfully made. Your works are wonderful; my soul knows this very well... Your eyes saw my unformed substance. In your book everything was written, the days that were planned for me, before they existed. How precious to me are your thoughts, God! How vast is their sum!" (Psalm 139:13-17)

The Father's plan for your life is not a plan that constrains you, it is one that makes sense of you. It incorporates the talents, abilities, desires, motivations, joys and pleasures that make you, "you"; gifts from the Father that reflect His hopes and thoughts for you.

Let's explore this idea naturally.

The Race to Run

There are two basic types[4] of muscle tissue in every skeletal muscle in our body. There are long thin fibres, Type 1, that are made for endurance work; and there are tightly packed bulky fibres, Type 2, that are made for explosive bursts of energy. It is your DNA, not exercise, that determines the proportion of these two types of tissue in your various muscles. If you exercise you will increase your overall muscle mass and the efficiency of these fibres, but they will increase in the same proportion of skinny endurance cells to bulky strength cells that you had to start with.

Sprinters tend to be made of mostly bulky strength tissue, while marathon runners are all skinny endurance tissue, and middle-distance runners have a mix of the two. So you have an optimum running distance determined by the gift of genetics. Whether or not you are fit enough to run your optimum distance is not the point, training will enable you to run any distance faster than not training. But it will not change the race to which you are genetically best suited to run.

"So ... let's also lay aside every burden and the sin that entangles us and let's run with endurance the race that is set out before us." (Hebrews 12:1b)

The race set out before us is unique to each of us. It suits our gifts. Its route is marked out in the days that the Father was planning and the thoughts He was thinking about us since before our uncomprehending eyes blinked at their first daylight and the pre-natal gifts He had knitted into us started to interact with the world to write our life story.

The plan the Father has for us doesn't dictate the story; we have to write the story with our choices and actions. His love for us leaves us lots of freedom. But it also provides a framework and structure to our lives. He has set a race for each of us that brings all our pieces together and makes them fit. He's marked the course, but we regularly miss or ignore the signs. Too often we decide that someone else's race looks easier or more interesting.

When I was seventeen I got my first paid job. I worked as a fly-man in the stage crew of the West End production of the musical "Bugsy Malone". Night after night four young gangsters would sing:

"We could have been anything that we wanted to be, with all the talent we had..."[5]

Now it's true that you can use your talents in any way you choose; gifts are *given* not just loaned. But it is seldom true that they are enough for you to be *whatever* you want to be.

The freedom to be anything we want actually leaves us as prisoners to our own limitations. Whereas using our gifts in co-operation with His plans for us can take us to extraordinary places that our talents alone never could have.

It is for freedom that Christ has set us free (Galatians 5:1), but paradoxically it is by submission that we experience that freedom.

God's plan is more like a game plan than a blueprint, a training programme to reveal His workmanship in us. The competitors in our race are not other people – they have their own races to run. Instead, our competitors are other versions of us; versions that for various reasons have picked up baggage along the way, or have become stuck in their own unredeemed nature or, for lack of vision, don't keep to the route (Proverbs 29:18). They are us going somewhere we were not called to go, trying to be someone we were not made to be.

This is a book about identity!

"But just one receives the prize? Run like that, to win!" (2 Corinthians 9:24b)

The burdens and entanglements of life tempt us to take routes better suited to who we have become, rather than who we were made to be. These routes may not be part of the Father's plan for us, but His precious thoughts towards us did anticipate these detours and He made contingencies for them.

Throughout life God will call and re-call us, sometimes to keep us on track, sometimes to bring us back on track, and sometimes to unlock the next phase of the life that belongs to us.

The Supra-Natural Life was a book about the process of change. It explored how Word and Spirit worked together in our formation. This book is about the discovery of the target of that change of His Word in you, not just how His words to you can change you.

By the end you should have a clearer vision of God's plan for your life: short, medium and longer-term; and the meaning and value in you revealed by that plan and calling; the rich glory of your inheritance in the saints.

Don't worry if you are not sure yet what your calling is or the hope beyond it. Knowing who you really are is never as straightforward as it seems it should be. Even if you do have some idea, stick with me, there is more ahead of you than you can yet see, which is why Paul prays for our hearts to be enlightened (see Ephesians 1:18).

We all need revelation, not just information, to see the truth in ourselves for ourselves!

What's in Your Hand?

There are potential stages in the life ahead of you that go way beyond what you could ask or think right now, so we will obviously need revelation for the future. But the journey into your future starts, as it did for Moses, by seeing what we already have in the natural, but in a supranatural way.

"And Moses answered back: 'What if...' And the Lord said to him

21

'What is that in your hand?' and he said, 'It is a rod'." (Exodus 4:1-2)

As a shepherd Moses had carried a rod for forty years, but his encounter with the Lord made it a symbol and resource for Moses' new calling to lead God's people out of Egypt. God had been preparing Moses for the calling ahead of him since before Moses' parents hid him in a floating basket, but it was only after this moment of revelation that we start to see how his life story made sense. The access to Pharaoh's court that came through his stepmother; the education, administrative and leadership skills his courtly upbringing gave him. Even Moses' forty years learning the ways of the desert, using a rod to lead his flocks from wadi to wadi. The skills, knowledge, relationships, failures and contradictions of Moses' early life all became relevant when God commissioned him at the burning bush.

One day, Moses' rod would become the stumbling block that prevented him stepping into the next phase of his calling (Numbers 20:7-12). Moses had confused the successes of calling with the hope of an inheritance beyond it. He boxed himself into a position, rather than releasing the person he could have been. But that's for later.

Calling starts with revelation that gives a supranatural purpose to what's in us naturally.

City of Angels

For an old friend of mine that enlightenment came mid-air and mid-Atlantic, via an angel on a flight from Heathrow to Los Angeles.

Kevan was working as an airline steward, but what Kevan really loved was music.

On this particular flight, a man with a South African accent called Kevan over and asked to speak with him privately. Without really thinking it through, Kevan agreed and brought him into the small stewards room, a room that was supposed to be off-limits to passengers. The man with the South African accent then told Kevan to quit his day job and pursue music full time.

Kevan was already a gifted musician. He had a home studio and had written commercial music that was used in corporate promotional videos and the like. He had played in several local bands, but being a professional musician hadn't paid enough. That was why he had taken the job with the airline in the first place.

The South African went on to tell Kevan things that Kevan has never shared with anyone else. Then he disappeared. Kevan is not quite sure how, he just wasn't there any more. During the rest of the flight Kevan searched the plane for him, but someone else was now sitting in the South African's seat.

Today Kevan is highly lauded in the music business as a producer, songwriter, Tony-nominated composer and musician. He's not well known outside his professional circle and being a musician has taken him to the edge of bankruptcy as well as providing a comfortable income. Kevan has been a pastor, evangelist, counsellor, comforter and friend to an array of well-known names on both sides of the Atlantic. People whose chaotic and sometimes-destructive lifestyles would normally have left them unconnected to the grace and peace that Kevan carries.

Sadly Kevan is often criticised for his association with projects and people that seem, and often are, godless. But revelation will take you on journeys religion will not. It will also help give you the courage needed to stay the course when people reject you; or call you foolish; and when the natural rewards dry up.

Kevan was able to respond as he did because of the gifts already in him. He was running the race he was best suited to.

Now there is also a work for us to do that we'll never be naturally qualified for, but Jesus normally leads us by a route that stretches our natural abilities first. Without revelation we would never guess the destiny He is calling us towards. But there are clues as to how to get there already in us.

Most of us will not be told by an angel what to do next in life, but

Jesus will call us. If He didn't, we would all be trapped within the limits of our own strength and vision, often in day jobs that pay the rent but frustrate the eternity in us (Ecclesiastes 3:11).

As we explored in the *The Supra-Natural Life*, the key is to live daily in every word He speaks to us (Matthew 4:4); living in it (John 8:31) and letting it live in us (John 15:7). Co-operating with the effective intervention of the Spirit in us (Romans 8:26-27) as we grow up into Christ and become co-heirs with Him.

Calling is just a special class of the words He speaks to us. They are the ones that are most positively and uniquely about us and our journey.

You need to hear His call directly as you read this book. You can't live on someone else's revelation, as the calling of Simon Peter so powerfully demonstrates.

"You Will Be Called 'Rocky'"

If we only had the synoptic Gospels it would seem that the first time Jesus met Simon and his brother Andrew they were willing to leave everything to answer His call. But in fact, John's Gospel tells us that they had already met each other near Jerusalem, under John the Baptist's ministry and teaching.

It was here that Andrew first heard John the Baptist describe Jesus as the "Lamb of God" and as the "Baptiser in the Holy Spirit". So Andrew finds Jesus and spends a day with Him. He then finds his brother Simon and tells him to come and meet "the Christ" (John 1:41). This was a big, faith-filled conclusion on Andrew's part based on a single day with Jesus.

Simon accepts his brother's invitation and as he meets Jesus for the first time, Jesus looks at him and prophesies:

"You are Simon the son of John, *you will be called 'Peter.'*" (John 1:42)

The first thing Jesus ever says to Simon is that one-day Simon will have a new nickname: "Peter" which means "Rocky" or "The Rock".

"Simon" on the other hand means "Listener" or "Hearer", which is ironic as Simon Peter is famous for being the only man in the Bible to be interrupted by all three members of the Trinity while he is still talking.[6]

Perhaps Jesus knew that Simon wasn't really ready to hear any more about his call to be "The Rock", so at this point Jesus stops. But Simon has at least listened to Andrew, his own flesh and blood, and as a result Simon gets to be at the wedding in Cana and at a feast in Jerusalem where he sees various signs and miracles.

So when Jesus arrives at the Sea of Galilee some months after their first meeting, Simon[7] is ready to respond to a simple call: "Follow me and I will make you fishers of men" (Mark 1:17).

Jesus has already caught Simon, so it is easy for Him to invite him to help catch others too. Jesus describes what He wants Simon to do in fishing terms that make sense of who Simon already is, but there is a hope beyond the immediate trip. It is the person God has always seen in Simon, the man he was made to be. But at this stage "Peter" is still in Simon's future. Time with Jesus will draw out this future hope.

Three years later, Jesus and His disciples are on a retreat in Caesarea Philippi and Simon is ready to let his future press into his present. Jesus asks Simon who he thinks He is and Simon replies that Jesus is "the Christ, the Son of the living God" (Matthew 16:16).

This time Jesus says:

"Well done, you are Simon Bar-Jonah because flesh and blood didn't reveal this to you but my Father who is in heaven did, and I say to you as well, you are 'Peter'! " (Matthew 16:17-18a)

The promise of Simon's initial meeting with Jesus, "you *will be* called 'Peter'", is beginning to become a present reality, "you *are* 'Peter'".

Simon has already learnt to bring who he is from an earthly perspective (Simon the fisherman) into co-operation with a divine calling as Simon the fisher of men. But from now it is heaven's

25

vision of Simon that will dominate and shape what he will do and be called. Simon becomes Peter the rock!

Let's unpack Jesus' reply and you will see what I mean.

The first time Simon had met Jesus it was Simon's literal flesh and blood, his brother Andrew, who told him that Jesus was the Christ. But on this occasion Simon, who occasionally listens, has just lived up to his parent's hopes for him in a spiritual way. They had named him "Simon"; the "Hearer" had just heard truth about Jesus directly from the Father.

Simon's earthly father was called "John", as Jesus acknowledged the first time they met (John 1:42 above), but this time Jesus calls Simon "bar-Jonah" which means "son of Jonah". This is not a misspelling, as some believe. Jonah was the only Old Testament prophet to come from Galilee[8] and, of course, as an amateur fisherman had the biggest you-should-have-seen-the-one-that-got-away story in history. Interestingly, Jonah was also an evangelist to the Gentiles, a task that lies in Peter's future too.

So Simon has an inheritance in Jonah, the Galilean prophet, because, just as God spoke to Jonah, Father in Heaven is revealing things to Simon too. But more than that, Jonah is also the only prophet to whom Jesus likens Himself. So Simon is becoming like someone who already reflected something of the life of Jesus, even before Jesus was born.

Christ in You is a Mystery!

In His reply, Jesus is highlighting in every way possible that revelation, not simply information, is changing something in Simon. Expanding Jesus' words with the meaning implicit in them, Jesus has just said:

"Well done, Mr Hearer, son of that fishy Galilean prophet who preached to the Gentiles and had his own resurrection experience, because unlike when we first met you didn't get this truth about me from your brother, but you have just heard it directly from my

Father in Heaven. So while you are open to revelation, I now have something to say about you! *You are Rocky...*"

Simon's openness to revelation about Jesus creates the opportunity to receive revelation about himself:

"...and on this rock I will build my church, and the gates of Hades shall not hold against it. And I will give you the keys of the Kingdom of Heaven and whatever you bind on Earth will have been bound in Heaven and whatever you loose on Earth will have been loosed in Heaven." (Matthew 16:18b-22)

Hearing a single sentence from the Father about Jesus released a whole paragraph of revelation from Jesus about Simon. "Peter" was Simon's "inheritance in the saints" (see Ephesians 1:18); the version of Simon that Jesus saw hidden inside him.

"You are Peter" spoke to Simon's identity, but it was also a word of grace, with the power to build up Simon (Acts 20:32). It was a word from Jesus, with the potential to fulfil Simon's desires (John 15:7). And it was a word from God, providing an opportunity for faith (Romans 10:17).

In the book of Acts and in Peter's letters we see this word in action in Peter – the rock. He becomes a foundation stone in the Church. He was its first leader (Acts 2:14); the first evangelistic preacher (Acts 2:21); and the first cross-cultural missionary (Acts 10:34+). He exercised the authority to bind and loose both in the Church (Acts 15:7-12) and over the occult powers that shaped secular society (Acts 8:20). By the time Peter writes his letters it is clear that he has thought long and hard about what it means to be a living rock in God's house (1 Peter 2:5-8).

Without this word from Jesus, Peter's future leadership and his exercise of authority, even his theological ruminations, would have been no more than speculative presumption, pride and self-promotion on Peter's part. But with the word, Peter's actions become submitted obedience to the gift and call in him.

Peter wasn't the only disciple to be given a new name or receive a promise when he first met Jesus. James and John are called "sons of thunder"; Philip is told he is "an Israelite without guile" (John 1:47); Nathaniel is promised that he would "see the heavens opened and the Angel's of God ascending and descending on the Son of Man" (John 1:51). It is just that we know more about how Jesus' words to Peter were fulfilled by him.

But Jesus also told us that: "many are called, but few are choice"[9] (Matthew 22:14), which is a Jewish way of saying, "Everyone has a calling, but only a few exhibit the quality of chosenness."

Jesus will have already spoken a key word into you about your calling, though you may well have missed it. We're not always ready to hear it or respond. But don't worry He'll speak it again when you're ready and in the meantime, as He did with Simon, He will call you in ways that make more natural sense right now to lead you into your future: "Okay Simon, come and be a fisher-of-men then."

The Jack and the Joker

In *The Supra-Natural Life* I mentioned how at age fifteen I was given a word about having a prophetic ministry, but that the word made no sense. It was beyond me, so I had dismissed it until just a few years ago when it suddenly became obvious, though not in the way most might think of the prophetic.

I must have been about seventeen years old the first time I actually recognised Jesus speaking to me about my identity in a way I could respond to. As with Simon, called to be a fisher-of-men at Galilee, Jesus spoke in terms that worked for me in a natural way.

At fifteen I had faced death for the third time in my life. I had an aggressive non-Hodgkin's lymphoma. Then, at sixteen I had been miraculously healed. This miracle, combined with a striving heart, made me very zealous for Jesus and leadership. My thought at the time was to quit education as soon as possible and become an evangelist. With hindsight there is some irony in this, in that while I've done lots of evangelism, it has definitely not been the most fruitful ministry gift in me.

So in my zeal I prayed about who I was supposed to be and what I was supposed to do. I guess I expected a slow answer over time, coming as advice via other people and verses in scripture. Instead I had a picture. I saw playing cards. They weren't any old playing cards, they were a decorative pack of Norwegian playing cards from my childhood. First I saw the Joker, then I saw it being played in a number of different poker hands, none of them particularly strong, but all of them winning. I remember thinking, "Oh, the Joker is the wild card." Then I heard the phrase, "Jack of all trades, master of none".

It wasn't difficult to understand what Jesus seemed to be saying. I was to play whatever part Jesus needed me to play in whatever situation I found myself in. There seemed to be a promise in the picture as well, in that the hands, while not remarkable, had become winning hands.

This "word" became a very accurate description of my life and ministry over the next two decades. Like Barnabus I have done the work of an evangelist, a pastor, a teacher, and I have even done the work of the prophet and apostle. I've been a kids' worker, a youth worker, an administrator, a project manager, a missions manager, an event planner and even a worship leader, despite my lack of musicality. Some of this just happened. But some of it happened because of my response to this word, both prayerfully and practically. I didn't forget about it, it became a topic in my prayer life that led me to take some roles based on the need of a team rather than my qualification for the task.

But a few years ago Jesus modified my understanding of this word. I don't remember how it came up, but out of the blue someone commented: "You know that phrase 'Jack of all trades, master of none', that's actually a cynical joke about shoddy builders. The phrase was originally, 'Jack of all trades, master of one'. It was the aspiration of novice tradesman who had to do everything while they became an expert in something."

It was impossible for me not to hear this information without thinking about the word I had carried in a loose way for a lot of years. Shortly afterwards I read the verse in Luke that says, "If you have not been faithful with what is someone else's, who will give you what is your own?" (Luke 16:12). I knew the Lord was speaking: I was stepping out of my apprenticeship, during which I had been whatever others needed me to be, and into a role in which I was a master craftsman as well as being a useful generalist.

Faith and Faithfulness

In the passage I just quoted from Luke's Gospel, Jesus actually gives three consecutive statements about the connection between faithfulness and the growth of what we have by faith. As I thought about them I realised that Jesus had also lived by them before He stepped into His public ministry. In other words, Jesus preached what He had already practised.

Jesus said:

"Whoever is faithful in the little things will also be faithful in much, and whoever is fickle[10] in the little things will also be fickle in much. And if you have not been faithful with fickle wealth, then who will trust you with the real thing? If you have not been faithful with what is someone else's, who will give you what is your own?" (Luke 16:10-12)

There are three principles here that will be true for everyone who walks in the life they are called to.

- Be faithful in the small things you already have and you will be trusted with lots more.
- Be faithful in the things by which the world measures worth and you will be trusted with the things that really have value.
- Be faithful in serving the life and calling entrusted to others and you will receive your own "inheritance in the saints".

Later we will specifically look at Jesus' childhood and young adult life, where we can see Him put these three principles into practice. But these three ideas also run right through this book. We will learn to love the gifts we already have from Father, to free ourselves from the way the world values us and to accept the Father's plan for us above our own ideas – often to discover that He wants to give us our desires anyway.

Faithfulness is simply the fullness of faith. To be faithful simply means that we consistently act in an area of life with faith, which is why I used the legitimate translation of "fickle" instead of "unfaithfulness" in the verse above. It's not just doing things in a bad or evil way that prevents us from growing, it is our inconsistency in doing them the right way.

We are also told that:

"Through faith, we understand that the ages have been framed by the word of God." (Hebrews 11:3)

While this verse is actually about how men and women of faith have moved world history forward, from epoch to epoch, it is also true for our personal history.

Some of the words Jesus speaks to us frame or demark the seasons of our life, the phases in the Father's plan. Faith can come by hearing these words of Christ (Romans 10:17), but faith is completed by our actions (James 2:22b). The principles in the Luke 16 passage above – faith in the small, faith with the world's value and faith with other people's things – may well be the substance of the faith that moves us through the phases of Father's plan for our lives.

These are the general truths of faith that move us all forward towards our inheritance whatever that might be. To become a master in whatever field – church, politics, education, business, family etc – the journey will be walked in the same way.

The Many and the Few
"Never... was so much owed by so many to so few." (Winston

Churchill, 20th August 1940)[11]

In *The Supra-Natural Life* we saw how creation is groaning, waiting for God's children to grow up into their inheritances (Romans 8:19-21).

While the many could walk in calling, as Jesus warns us, only the few do. But those who do are owed a huge amount by the rest of creation. The few have walked in every sphere of life and built something out of their passions and a promise from God. They have received an inheritance that will benefit their children's children in this world. They have written a story that will be told in eternity, though it's likely they'll be forgotten in this life. But that's for the end of this book.

Right now we need to hear Peter's advice:

"Be diligent to make your calling and election sure." (2 Peter 1:10a)

We saw in Simon's call that information from other people is not revelation unless the Spirit has breathed through it and even then, "the word of His grace which has the power to build you up", won't do so unless you give it attention and space.

So I'd like you to be diligent in taking time to process what you've read with the Holy Spirit. I suggest you have something with which to makes notes as you talk to Jesus, the margins of this book are a start. Summarise the thoughts it provokes in you and write down any questions it has raised. And give time for Jesus to speak back to you.

As a guide, why not think about how you first met Jesus. Was there anything at the time that stood out, something that might have been Him speaking to you? Don't worry if you can't remember anything; as with Simon, Jesus will come back to it.

Since then, have you been aware of any words given to you by others or that you have felt, heard or seen for yourself? Again, ask Jesus to help you remember.

What are your natural skills and what do you like doing?

Finally, take time to ask if Jesus wants to say anything right now! If you hear or remember anything, write it down so you can come back to it as we build up a picture of the plan Father has for you.

Endnotes

2. Famously spoken by the character Maximus in the film Gladiator.

3. We explored the implications of man's dual nature, mud and glory, more fully in *The Supra-Natural Life*.

4. In humans, Type 2 fibres have two different sub-types. There are also two further types of non-skeletal muscle tissue found in reflex muscles like the heart.

5. Story by Alan Parker, music and lyrics by Paul Williams.

6. Simon Peter is interrupted by the Father on the Mount of Transfiguration, Matthew 17:4-5; by the Son whilst mid-rebuke, Matthew 16:22-23; and by the Holy Spirit in the house of Cornelius, Acts 10:44.

7. The Gospels all still call Simon-Peter "Simon" at this point, though Matthew's Gospel, written for a later audience, flags that Simon and Peter are the same person.

8. Jesus knows that Simon's father is called "John". He has used this name in the past, see John 1:42 above.

9. Most English translations use the word "chosen" for the Greek word "eklectos", but a quick review of the word as it is used in the Septuagint, the Greek version of the Old Testament, will demonstrate that the word is actually about the quality that gets an item selected, not the act of selection. So some translators use the word "choice" which is a more accurate translation, though it can seem strange when read in English.

10. Although the Greek word "adikos " is normally translated as "unrighteous" or "unjust", it is used here in contrast to "faithfulness". In its positive form the root "dikos" is connected to the verb "deiknuo" which means literally "to show" or to "expose to the eyes" and is used metaphorically to mean "to demonstrate" or "to prove". In that light the word "fickle" seems a good translation in this situation to emphasise its untrustworthy or inconsistent quality.

11. "The few" were the RAF pilots, often just out of college, whose sacrifice prevented the early invasion of the United Kingdom and won the Battle of Britain.

CHAPTER 2

THE IDIOT'S TALE AND THE

OVERCOMER'S STORY

"The start of the Gospel of Jesus Christ, the Son of God." (Mark 1:1)

These are the opening words of the first Gospel to be written down. Mark redefined the word "Gospel". In the ancient world a Gospel was the pronouncement of a reward[12] or a favour; often it came attached to news of a victory or of peace after a war. Mark's Gospel had all the elements of a regular Gospel: favour, rewards, victory and peace. But Mark's Gospel came in the form of a story, a biography. And that was new.

A story acts as an interface between someone's words and actions, and a bigger context. That bigger context reveals the meaning of events and the identity of the characters in the story. We understand Jesus not simply in the individual things He said and did, but in the story His life wrote. The telling of this story has changed the world (Mark 16:15-20).

A story helps us answer the questions "who am I?" and "what

should I do now?" Mark seems to understand this and so right in the middle of His biography Jesus poses the question: "And who do you say that I am?" (Mark 8:29).

Without a story you can't know who you are!

Sadly most people neither experience their own existence as a story nor see how their day-to-day activity plays a part in a bigger narrative. For most, life unfolds as a series of monotonous cycles, disjointed accidents and random events. A tedium of time and tides.

"The sun rises; the sun sets... The wind blows South, then turns North... Rivers run to the sea, but the sea is not full... It's all tedious beyond words." (Ecclesiastes 1:5-8)

But a story lays purpose on to what would otherwise be just the pedestrian passing of time and motion. The main characters in a great novel or film seem to achieve a significance that goes beyond the individual moments of their lives. Their place in a bigger narrative gives them a bigger meaning and defines who they are.

And so we all try to connect to a bigger story by the things we do. For some, that story is history. We look to do something that will leave a mark and a remembrance beyond ourselves. So we create art, write books, have children, carve our names onto trees, sow ourselves into causes or lead unconventional lives just to stand out from the crowd. Anything to let the world know, for as long as possible, that we have been here.

The things we do in life might not quite echo in eternity, but they should at least chime loud in this life and, with luck, resound in our legacy.

But history is a forgetful narrator:

"For of the wise, just as of the fool, there is no lasting memory, since in days to come all will have been long forgotten." (Ecclesiastes 2:16a)

Two and half thousand years after the author of Ecclesiastes wrote these words, the French Philosopher Jean-Paul Sartre came to the same conclusion.

"All human actions are equivalent and all are on principle doomed to failure. So it amounts to the same thing whether one gets drunk alone or is the leader of nations."[13]

If we are looking to any sort of history (family, local or global) to give our lives real meaning, we will ultimately be disappointed. Kingdoms rise and kingdoms fall and the next wave washes away the footprints of the last.

As Shakespeare so eloquently says through the character Macbeth, a man who goes to the extremes of murder and war to become a somebody...

"Life's a walking shadow, a poor player that struts and frets its hour upon the stage and then is heard no more. It is a tale told by an idiot, full of sound and fury, signifying nothing."[14]

All of these great thinkers were correct in their logic, but wrong in their perspective. They all wrote from a natural perspective or, as the author of Ecclesiastes describes it, they all considered life "under the sun".

"So I thought about all my activity, the things I had put my hand to and the efforts of my work. And I saw it was all empty and striving after the wind. *There is no value under the sun*." (Ecclesiastes 2:11)

Fortunately, the life Jesus came to give us is not one to be lived from a natural perspective. It is above the natural, *supra*natural. It is life *under heaven*.

Life under heaven has times and seasons to it!

"A man's steps are laid out by the Lord, who delights in the journey." (Psalm 37:23)

There are God-authored life-steps that reflect the Father's pre-natal excitement and thoughts about us (see Psalm 139:17 in the last chapter).

Under Heaven
Ecclesiastes is really an incredibly positive book, but it has a

reputation for being depressing and negative. Its author, the Preacher Teacher (Ecclesiastes 1:1) paints a beautiful picture in contrasts of black and gold. Most of the book is written from the perspective of under the sun, and from here his verdict is all bleak, black and grey. But every now and again the Preacher pulls back a veil to let the glory of heaven shine onto our earth-bound activity. From the perspective of "under heaven", even the simplest of activities can be washed in gold. Under heaven, the tedious cycles of chapter one (see Ecclesiastes 1:5-8 "above") become the purposeful seasons of chapter three (see Ecclesiastes 3:1-8 "below").

"There is a due season for everything and a time for every purpose under heaven. A time to be born and a time to die; A time to plant and a time to uproot; A time to kill and a time to heal; A time to pull down and a time to build; A time to cry and a time to laugh; A time mourn and a time to dance; A time to throw away and a time to gather; A time to hug and a time to shun; A time to look for and a time to lose; A time to keep and time to discard; A time to tear and a time to sew; a time to keep quiet and a time to speak up; A time to love and a time to hate; A time for war and a time for peace." (Ecclesiastes 3:1-8)

From the perspective of heaven everything has a due season. Any action can connect to God's purpose, it's just a matter of timing and relationship. Even a simple life can have meaning under heaven as a gift from God:

"...and that man who eats and drinks and sees good in his own activity, it is God's gift." (Ecclesiastes 3:13)

In contrast, under the sun even the most worthy activity is "empty, empty..." no matter how grand the schemes or how far the extremes.

"...it is all empty" (Ecclesiastes 1:2)

Or as Sartre put it in the twentieth century:

"Life has no meaning the moment you lose the illusion of being eternal." But eternity is not an illusion. Our problem is that, too often we can't see the connection between a day at the office and the eternal thoughts of God for us. If we're going to see it for ourselves we probably need to see it more fully in Jesus' life first. We will start with a single incident, a transition point where one phase of God's plan for His Son gave way to the next.

The Greatest Story Ever Told

Mark starts his version of Jesus' story at the Jordan. It is the moment when Jesus, the private artisan, becomes a public figure.

When Jesus arrived at the Jordan He was "builder"; when He left He was "preacher-teacher", just like the writer of Ecclesiastes.

At the Jordan, Jesus' identity didn't change, but it was time for a new season under heaven so the focus of Jesus' calling changed. There was a new work prepared for Him to do: preaching and teaching.

People found the change hard to accept.

"He began to *teach* in the synagogue; and many listeners were astounded saying: 'where did He get these ideas, what is this wisdom....Isn't this the *builder* the son of Mary?'" (Mark 6:3)

Tradition has translated the Greek word "tekton" in this verse "carpenter" rather than "builder". Perhaps because it felt more honouring to think of Jesus as a private artisan with His own workshop than as a builder jobbing His way around Palestine. But the word "tekton" is more properly "builder".[15] This is more than just a point about words, there is a wealth of understanding that falls into place when we realise that Jesus was a builder before He became a teacher. But we can only scratch the surface of it here.

At the moment, I am only interested in the change of season that the Jordan represented in Jesus' life, so although the words and actions of the Father and Holy Spirit have a lot to say about Jesus' identity and His calling in the phase about to start, I just want to point out that we know that Jesus had been faithful in the life He had led to that point – because His Father is "well pleased" with Him (Matthew 3:17b) and "without faith it's impossible to be well pleasing to Him" (Hebrews 11:6).

As a builder Jesus was faithful with the natural gifts and provisions of His earthly context. He had faithfully served His earthly father's calling until His father's death. These are two out of three of Jesus' growth principles from the last chapter. Be faithful in the little, be faithful with what belongs to another.

But what I really want to draw out was how excited the Father was about the life He had planned for His Son. He was excited that He had so subtly hidden in plain sight details about His plans for Jesus' life – and this transition in particular – that the vast majority of Jesus' followers had never seen them.

To draw them out we need to learn a bit of ancient Hebrew and a bit of an even older language, Akkadian.

Adam, the Fruitful Builder

Now you probably know that Adam means "man" and you may well know that it also means "red" and is connected to the Hebrew word for earth, "adamah". People sometimes join the two words and translate Adam's name as something catchy like "Red Earthling" which sounds a bit sci-fi, but the alternative, "Muddy Red", sounds like a blues musician, so you can take your pick.

For a long time scholars have pointed out that Adam wasn't Jewish and didn't speak Hebrew. In fact, he appears as the first man in other ancient writings, such as the Assyrian creation legends. In these his name is "Adamu" which is a proper word in the oldest language we know anything about, Akkadian. In Akkadian, "Adamu" means to "produce", "make" or "build" and if translated actively the name "Adam" means "Producer", "Maker" or "Builder".[16]

This is interesting, because the first Adam was a gardener, which makes him a producer; and the last Adam, Jesus (1 Corinthians 15:45), was a builder. So Adam is a producer-maker-builder.

Things are about to get more interesting, but first I want to go back briefly to the word "neshemah" from the start of the last chapter: the breath of God in us. It's a bit technical but it completes our understanding.

Hebrew words are constructed by extending a two or three letter root word with extra letters that modify the root's basic meaning. At the heart of the word "neshemah" is the root "shem", four letters in English but only two in Hebrew: "Sh-M". On its own "shem" is translated as the English word "name". But as a root, it really carries the idea of the fundamental essence of something, the distilled quality, the nature or identity that makes a thing or person what it is. So God breathed a gust of His essence, "neshemah", into His earth-formed image and it became a prophetic name, "shem", in him "Adam", the producer-maker-builder.

Being a builder was not just any old job for Jesus. Vocationally, being a builder expressed something in Jesus' essence that made Him the second Adam. Prophetically there is more to Jesus being a builder than just this connection with Adam, but we will come to that.

Just one last bit of Hebrew: the word for "Heaven", "Shamayim", is a plural noun that starts with this same root "Sh-M". Because Heaven is the place of essences, it is the place of names; it is the place from which every meaningful purpose flows.

This is why there can be a season for every purpose *under heaven*. Whereas *under the sun*, life is always an idiot's tale, however much sound and fury it generates.

We may know only a little about Jesus' life as a builder, but He spent more than four-fifths of His life doing this job and I would suggest that it was as much part of a divine plan as His ministry years. In fact, I can show you that it was.

The Thoughts of Heaven
Luke records Jesus' family tree for us all the way back to God

through Adam. The list contains some wonderful names in it; names that prophetically anticipate Jesus. Names like "Shelah", which is "Peace"; "Arphaxad", which probably means "Healer" or "Releaser"; and "Nahor", which means "Light" (though the same word can also mean "Snorter" which doesn't seem so wonderful). It was in noticing these names that I started to wonder if there was something more to them and I discovered that you could make prophetic sentences out of the names of Jesus' ancestors.[17]

In particular, the names from God to Noah read like this:[18]

"God (Elohim) Man (Adam) is appointed (Seth) a mortal man (Enosh), sorrowful/begotten (Kenen[19]); the glory of God (Mahalalel[20]) descends (Jared) to dedicate/a teacher (Enoch[21]), his death shall bring (Methuselah) the depraved/humble man (Lamech[22]) rest (Noah)."

I've kept the sentence quite raw because I want the simple facts to speak for themselves. Translating names is a tricky business, but all the options above come from standard credible sources. I've added some comments in the endnotes to explain why I have preferred one option over another for certain names, and for others I've given two meanings because both seem significant.

Now we also saw above, that there is more in the name Adam than simply "Man" or even "Red Earthling".

So the prophetic sentence hidden in the names of Jesus' ancestors from chapters one to six of the Bible and from the dawn of history reads:

"God a/the producer-maker-builder is appointed a mortal man/begotten/of sorrow. The glory of God descends to dedicate/a teacher, his death shall bring the humble/depraved rest."

Don't you just love the word of God!

Now I want you to see just how subtly this hidden prophecy matches Jesus' life story. Because it tells us something about the shape of the Father's plan for every human life. Jesus' life story is the model for all of us.

Jesus' family-line-prophecy hints at three entangled but progressive phases to the Father's plan for Jesus:

First, **"God a/the producer-maker-builder is appointed a mortal man (begotten) of sorrow"**:

It is a bit ambiguous whether God is the builder being appointed or if He is appointing a builder to be a mortal man of sorrow. In Jesus, of course, both are true: Jesus the builder is also "Emmanuel", "God-with-us", but in the form of a mortal man.

Now the mortal life that Jesus lived as a builder was marked by grief, from the babies slaughtered because of His birth, through the two thousand Galileans crucified over Passover during Jesus' childhood, to the death of His earthly father. In the years of Jesus' youth He was "a man of sorrows, acquainted with grief" (Isaiah 53:2-3).

There is something here that relates to all of us. We are all born with natural gifts that reflect the image and essence of God in us, but into a painful world under a death sentence.

But we mustn't forget the positive in this first phase of Father's plan: the producer-maker-builder was appointed. Heaven's appointment gave Jesus' building activity eternal purpose. As Jesus grew He had a favour that was recognised as being heavenly in origin, even before He became a prophetic teacher. While still a builder, the Bible tells us:

"Jesus grew in wisdom and stature, and in favour with God and men." (Luke 2:52)

This first phase in Jesus' life is mirrored by those who walk in their calling. There is a fruitful heaven-appointed role for you to walk in, but you'll need to overcome some pains and disappointments too.

In this first phase we are called to do what should come naturally, because it's part of who we are. But we're to do it supranaturally, by faith and revelation, so that the grace Father pours onto us sticks to us as favour. We saw this phase of walking in calling in Kevan's story in the last chapter.

But the prophecy in Jesus' family tree goes on. After this producing, making, building phase, **"The Glory of God descends to dedicate/a teacher"**:

Now you have to understand the place of Enoch in Jewish culture (Enoch is the name behind the alternative translations, "to dedicate" and "a teacher"). In the Bible, Enoch was famous for ascending to be with God and prophesying the flood through his son's name. Recognised as the first prophet-teacher, Jewish literature portrayed Him as a worker of miracles and a teacher of deep knowledge, a model of what Jesus would be after the Glory of God had descended on Him at His baptism.

There are phases of anointed calling that some followers of Jesus press into. They tend to come after a phase of faithful natural calling. Phases of anointed calling are characterised by new abilities and regular miraculous interruptions from Heaven.

Finally, there would be a phase of impact beyond Jesus' mortal limits: **"His death shall bring the humble/depraved, rest."**

Jesus' death bought peace or comfort to those humble enough to accept it, however depraved they had been. In this final phase Jesus fulfilled His prophetic name, "Salvation".

Now Hebrews chapter eleven makes the point that all the heroes who have walked by faith received their final testimony, promise and inheritance after their death. There is actually a way of facing death having already died to ourselves that releases a legacy for our children's children. Jesus calls it "fruit that remains" (John 15:16).

Hidden in the names of Jesus' forebears is a simple story that in broad terms reveals the phases or seasons of the called life. Of course, in any particular life there will be lots of loops and sub-sections as well, but if you press on in the upward call of God you will experience seasons that reflect these broad phases.

There's a time to discover the essence and prophetic truth in you; a time to overcome the rubbish life throws at you; a time to know favour on your natural gifts and talents; a time of anointing, that brings new truth, gifts and breakthrough; and a time to fall into the earth and be multiplied.

But something to note through all these phases is that there is a thread of spiritual warfare. We are formed in a broken world full of sorrow and our death in Christ will be part of the devil's defeat.

The discovery and taking of God's steps in your life is actually a thrilling and delightful journey, but it's a powerful and serious business at the same time. So we need to be aware of the battle over our lives.

The Overcoming Testimony

"They overcame him (the devil) by the blood of Lamb, and the word of their testimony, and that they didn't love their souls,[23] even to death." (Revelation 12:11)

This is an astounding statement. In the closing chapters of history Satan, the protagonist since before the beginning, is defeated by the telling of your story as well as by the blood of Jesus.

Now the cross was not just a moment in time. It was a price paid since before the foundations of creation (Revelation 13:8). It is a wound whose scar Jesus will carry forever (Revelation 5:6).

In the Cross, eternity collides with history.

As Jesus' blood dripped down from His crushed body, it seeped into the dirt of creation, the elements from which man is made, then the earth shook (Matthew 27:51); the sun went dark (Luke 23:44); death was broken open (Matthew 27:52); and the veil that separated man from God was ripped in two (Matthew 27:51, Mark 16:38, Luke 23:44).

That is the power of "the blood of the Lamb". By it, earth is anchored to heaven. And by it our stories become testimonies, the stories that connect life's sound and fury to the eternal love of God; testimonies are the tales that give meaning to the minutia of life.

The intimacy that the cross has won for me means that I can involve the God of creation in the food I'm going to eat, the games

I'm going to play, the music I'm going to listen to, as well as the battles I'm going to win with Him. And Father doesn't just listen, He gets involved. Together we start writing a story in the blood of Jesus that becomes too compelling an evidence for the devil's accusations to stand, either against us or against God.

At the deepest moment of his life's disaster, Job's wife suggests he "curse God and die" (Job 2:9), but Job holds on for a God who would rather die than leave him cursed. Job's testimony unravels the devil's accusation (Job 2:4-5).

Now the devil is not stupid and he has read the verse from Revelation about his defeat by Jesus' blood and by our testimonies. He can't do anything about the blood of Jesus, so we should not be surprised to discover that a core activity of the devil in people's lives is to keep their testimonies as short as possible. He wants you to do as much life as possible without using the access to Heaven that the cross has given you.

The devil will contest our lives at all its defining moments, to obscure God's plan over us. If we can't see God's plan we will not feel His care and attention and we'll treat our access as a backup plan and get on with life in our own strength.

We'll feel the emptiness, of course, and start striving for success by achievement. But the bigger our sacrifice the further away God will feel when achieving doesn't bring us any closer to Him. The key, of course, is to live in the opposite direction.

My hope is that you start to see more of the care and love of God in your life. It's easy in the good times, a challenge to rise to in the most disastrous and pointlessly tragic of times, but easy to miss in the day to day. But perhaps it's in the day to day that a testimony is more powerful, since we have leant on Jesus when we could have leant on our own solutions.

And as revelation brings light on all aspects of life, you'll start seeing just how Jesus is fitting all the random bits of it together to make you "you" in a new way.

Perhaps it is helpful to think about these things: your tastes; your joys; your sadnesses; the things that have happened to you; the things you've done; the friends you have met; the natural gifts you have; the skills you have learnt; your hopes and motivations ... as bits of coloured glass being fitted together to make a stained glass window. A lot of the pieces will have been broken over the years; it is a consequence of being born into a broken world. Some of the pieces can be used as they are, others might need re-breaking or re-shaping. But in the hands of a great craftsman, even the most misshapen and fractured pieces of glass can be given a setting that expresses beauty and meaning within the whole.

This is what your testimony looks like.

Of course, however good the design when finished, it is still only when the sun shines through it that we really see the genius of the artisan. Like a window in a grand cathedral, Jesus will uniquely produce His image from the seemingly random elements that are uniquely us. And then He gives us His glory to shine through the re-worked pieces of our lives. This is your testimony, the vision of you that glorifies your Creator and eternal Redeemer.

Taking Back the Stolen Past

A few days ago I was ministering at an international missions base in the UK. I was praying prophetically over people and came to one particular couple. The Lord showed me a need, which I asked them about and they confirmed it. But then, as I started to pray, I found myself saying to the wife, Immaculee:

"The Lord is re-writing your story, including the trauma. He is putting new value and meaning into it. He cannot change the events of the past, but He will change their meaning and use them."

After I had prayed the husband, Richard, told me enthusiastically that they had just completed writing down his wife's story.[24] I discovered that she had gone through the most awful trauma during the Rwandan civil war and genocide. As a couple they had felt the Lord say that by writing down the story they would be able to see Him in it more clearly and the Lord would be able to use it to help others.

I didn't ask for any other details of the wife's experiences, but as I have reflected on what she was doing I have realised that she was being very deliberate in her spiritual warfare. She was going back into the enemy's territory to take back for Jesus what had been stolen from her: her story! By taking back her story, she was living out Paul's advice to the Ephesian Church on how to take off the old version of herself and to put on the new:

"Put away... the old you... and put on the new, who in the likeness of God has been formed in righteousness and true holiness... Be angry but don't sin. Don't let the sun go down on your wrath, nor give place to the devil." (Ephesians 4:22-27)

The new "you" is being formed in a different environment from the old you – one of righteousness and holiness – which has no place of authority for sin or the devil. The new "you" is being formed in the place of dialogue with Jesus.

The Greek word for "place" in the verse above is the word for a specific location rather than just a general space. In the course of our lives there are specific incidents and places that seem to belong to the devil, he owns them. Many of them are transitions that were forced on us or ones we made out of a misshaped view of ourselves.

In these verses, Paul uses a specific example to illustrate how the enemy gets ownership of a location in our life: something happens to us which is part of the enemy's intent, not God's plan, and we are rightly angry (Ephesians 4:26). But legitimate anger becomes a brooding and unfocused wrath,[25] which we then let slip out of the light (the sun goes down on it). When this happens, the sin against us becomes sin in us. We take a turn on the journey where there isn't one on Father's route map. We go off road to take unplanned and difficult terrain.

Professional counsellors recognise a phenomenon they call "transference". With transference, a person has an unfocused, underlying emotional state that will transfer its attention to inappropriate events and people as life progresses. What counsellors recognise in extreme cases is actually pretty common in milder versions. Legitimate emotions have become unfocussed and inappropriate, operating in our lives from dark corners away from the sun.

By writing down her story, this missionary lady was putting away the old and putting on the new, taking back specific locations from the enemy by bringing them back into the light. In the light you can focus your emotions accurately and there is no sin in anger at injustice. But transferred anger at everyone who annoys us will rob us of our testimony. And for many, the hidden anger takes on a passive-aggressive role with the God who, deep down, they believe must have planned something horrible for them, perhaps to teach them a lesson they never asked to learn.

But wherever we have been, once emotions and events are back in the light and correctly lined up, Jesus can lead us into heart victory at every place in our story. He can take ownership back by putting truth back into our heart life.

Write the Vision Down

Now, I'm not saying here that we need go back over life with a fine-tooth comb to achieve forgiveness for sins or even to be healed from hurts. Jesus can do all these things in us without our specific knowledge of what He is doing. But Jesus values our stories. They have made us who we are and Jesus has valued us with His own blood, so it seems that He wants to involve us in this redemption process. It is honouring to us for Him to show us who we are and involve us in our own story development and redemption.

The locations in our history that belong to the devil and the emotional turbulence they create in our souls are like background noise, static on the radio that makes it so much harder to pick out the signals and messages from heaven. But once reclaimed it becomes so much easier to join the dots and see a picture of ourselves emerging that doesn't look like it was painted by Picasso racing a camel.

Releasing your full testimony will require change in your inner life. God shows Himself strong in those whose hearts are completely His (2 Chronicles 16:9). Whether consciously or unconsciously, we do need to have heart victories at the defining locations of our life-stories so far.

It is the seasons of life and their transitions that tell a life story. The changes of seasons are often the junctions in the journey. Some of the changes just happen. Others are forced on us. Some we choose. Take Jesus' life. If we were to map it out it might be something like this:

Jesus was born in Judea; moved to Egypt; returned to Galilee as a private artisan; went to the Jordan to be baptised; returned as a public figure; He taught for three years; then He forced a show down with the religious and political leaders in Jerusalem; He was executed; rose again; ascended; and sat down.

Of course, we could take any one of these seasons and break it down further, but however we define the story there are questions to ask of the events we choose to tell it by: "What does Jesus have to say about this?" or "How does this fit with the Father's plan for my life?"

Most of us will not write out our life's story in great detail as Immaculee and Richard have done. But I do believe that Jesus wants us to become more familiar with it, to discover His presence, purpose and victory in all its seasons and transitions. As you read through this book I want to help you develop an understanding of your own story and testimony, so I will ask you to write things down and to look for revelation both for your story and from it.

Whether you see it yet or not, there is colour and beauty in the pieces of your life so far and there are events yet to happen that can connect meaning and significance to past defeats, victories and even the trivia. So ask the Holy Spirit to help you to see your story and to show you how Jesus has been involved with your journey since before you were born.

Occasionally, you'll remember painful events and places. Don't ignore these places, but don't blame Jesus for them and don't leave them to the devil. Where there has been a battle over you there is always space for a heart victory, so ask Jesus to help you find it.

Before moving on, why not sketch out the major seasons and transitions of your life so far: when and where were you born? Where have you lived? Who are the important people in your life and how do you know them? How were you educated? What battles have you had to overcome? What are you good at and what do you enjoy?

Look at the list you've created and talk to the Lord about it. Ask Him to show you where He was in each situation and if there is anything He wants to say into each.

There's no need to be too detailed yet, we have six more chapters to go!

Endnotes

12. Ironically, the Greek version of the Old Testament actually uses the word "gospel" to describe the surprise execution of a messenger who had expected a reward or favour.

13. From "Being and Nothingness", published 1969.

14. Macbeth, Act 5, Scene 5.

15. An "architekton" was a "master builder", from which we derive the English word "architect".

16. See "Adam" in the "Catholic Encyclopedia, 1914"; or "The Old Testament in the Light of the Historical Records and Legends of Assyria and Babylonia" by T.G Pinches, 1903.

17. I've since discovered others are doing the same, though many of the sentences you find on the Internet seem to be a bit free and easy with what counts as a legitimate translation of an ancient name.

18. If you go online you will now find other derivations of this prophecy, but I've stuck to the way I first found it, following up a hunch based on the qualities prophesied in later names already mentioned.

19. Kenen has multiple possible meanings. Many commentaries will simply see the name as a derivation of Cain, but it is better to see its connection to the root of words such as the noun "qina" which is a lament or sad poem, hence the translation "sorrowful".

20. Some biblical dictionaries will translate this name as "Praise to God", but the "halal" part of the name primarily means to shine or flash. It is used of the sun and stars. If we assume the shining is towards God (the "el" at the end of the name) then the name would mean "Glory to God". But if we assume the shining is from God we get simply "Glory of God".

21. Enoch comes from the root "chanak" which means to "train up", "dedicate" or "initiate". Enoch was seen in Rabbinic traditions as the first anointed teacher from God, evidenced by his prophesying the coming flood by naming his son "Methuselah" ("His death shall bring it") and quoted by Jude in the new Testament as prophesying Jesus (Jude 14).

22. Lamech: comes from two Hebrew words: "Le", which means "to go towards" and "Muk" which is "low". So literally, someone who "goes low", this could mean depraved or it could mean humble. There are Lamechs in Genesis, one bad and one good, so perhaps both are covered. The one in Jesus' lineage is the good one.

23. "Soul" is the more usual translation of the Greek word "psuche" from which we get the English word "psyche".

24. Since writing this, the story has been published under the title: "Under His Mighty Hand".

25. The Greek word translated "wrath" is "parorgizo". Literally, this means "anger alongside", so it is anger that is not focused on a specific offence.

CHAPTER 3

BORN INTO CAIN

"We are His workmanship, created in Christ Jesus for good works, which God prepared before that we would walk in them." (Ephesians 2:10)

The first phase of God's plan for your life is to overcome the death and sorrow you were born into in order to live faithfully in the image and essence with which He has gifted you. In this chapter and the next we will explore the battle from birth to breakthrough to walk in the fruitful truth of who you are, not just generically as a child of God, but specifically you as "you".

It's the phase of calling described by the ancestors of Jesus from God the Father to Kenan.

"God, the producer-maker-builder, is appointed a mortal man begotten of sorrow."

The first call on your life is to overcome the pains and conflicts of life and the sentence of death over you, to become fruitful with the gifts and value in you. Since Cain, every one of us has been born in pain into an environment where sin is predatory.

"Then the Lord said to Cain ... sin is crouching at your door, it craves you, but you must master it."[26] (Genesis 4:7)

Cain's struggle with sin had actually started years before this, it started in the womb.

God had told Eve that the enmity between her and the snake meant she would bring forth children in pain or hurt (Genesis 3:16). The word for "pain" in this verse can also mean "offence". It's Cain's feeling of offence with God that leads him to murder his brother and miss his calling.

Cain was born mortal, begotten of sorrow.

A Matter of Life and Birth

Two Christmases ago, my old employer emailed me out of the blue. Paul was a Christian; he had been called on Boxing Day by one of his salesmen. Although not an active believer, Clive, the salesman wanted someone to pray with him as his pregnant wife had gone into hospital on Christmas Day and then slipped into a coma. She had swine flu.

Some readers will remember the UK swine flu outbreaks in 2009 and 2010. Swine flu is almost always fatal to pregnant mothers and as she deteriorated the hospital had called Clive in to "say goodbye" to an unconscious Liz. A machine was doing her breathing for her. That was the point at which Clive decided he wasn't going to lose her and their unborn baby without doing something. So he prayed and then thought to call Paul, who was probably more used to praying than he was, and Paul emailed me.

Although she was in a hospital some miles away, I knew I wanted to pray for Liz in situ and not just from a distance. The next day I drove with Paul and his son Michael to the hospital. We went into the intensive care ward in pairs to pray for Liz. Within hours of leaving, Liz started breathing for herself and then she came round.

The hospital induced a controlled coma, as it was important that Liz didn't put any stress on her lungs, she was still in a critical condition. I went back to the hospital a few days later with my wife, Judith, to pray for Liz again. While there, Judith prophesied that angels would be telling her it was time to return home.

Liz continued to improve until a month later we received the following email from Clive:

"Hi Everyone.

As you might have heard, Liz came home from hospital last Friday night. It was a surprise for all of us as we did not expect it to be quite so soon...

Nationally, Liz is apparently quite a unique case; there are not many pregnant women who have been through what she has and survived. It is therefore more poignant (that) she (is) telling me that when they removed the sedation, she remembers four angels around her bed who told her it was time to wake up. She was not aware she had been at the top of the prayer charts when she told me."

In May a healthy little girl, Lily Katherine Alice, was born.

Even in the 21st century the womb is statistically still the most dangerous place on earth to be. Every birth is a struggle and every life an adventure and a testimony waiting to happen. That you are here already makes you an overcomer and a miracle. But like most miracles, it's easy to take for granted as time moves on. The circumstances, the hopes, prayers, failures and victories of our birth are still carried by each one of us, whether we remember them or not.

My own life started with a struggle that I'm sure was not in God's plan for me. While in the birth canal I put my arms behind my back and got stuck. For four hours my mother and I were in a critical state. I was almost delivered but unable to move. The midwives called a doctor. As it became clear this was a serious situation my Dad, who was not allowed in the delivery room, got people praying. Then the doctor had the idea of using the forceps to push me backwards instead of pulling me forward. Somehow I untangled myself.

I only found out about my traumatic birth years later when someone else was praying for me in another life threatening situation, an inoperable, unresponsive non-Hodgkin's lymphoma. While praying they had a picture of me, naked and in darkness with my hands bound behind my back and then a light had come on. My mother recognised the reference straight away. She saw both the similarity of the enemy's assignment against my life and the promise implicit in the victory of my birth. My healing from cancer at the age of fifteen has, of course, been one of the defining moments in my own story.

But going back to that first struggle, the doctors needed to treat my mother after I was born, so I was put into a glass-sided cot and left on my own. For the first few days of my life I was separated from my mother, with minimal contact. I don't know precisely how these things affected my pliable newborn psyche, but it did something to me.

Growing up people would tell me that I seemed detached; emotionally self- sufficient; stoical and even unfriendly. A girlfriend, a guy I worked with, an old mentor, and even my wife, had all told me over the years that I was a watcher rather than a participator. I wasn't shaken by their verdict, just mildly interested that I was different from them. I could even see advantages to my emotional shape. But the truth was, I had been "twisted in iniquity" even in the victory of my survival at birth.

David, who in Psalm 139 knew the goodness of God's plan for his life from conception (see the first chapter), also knew that the battle with sin starts in the womb too. Sin entangles and contests the plans and designs God has for us. It distorts the truth in us even before we are born.

"See I was twisted[27] in iniquity and my mother incubated me[28] in sin. See You (God) desire truth in the innermost being" (Psalm

51:5-6a). The Bible never says we are all born "with" sin, but it does say we are "incubated", or literally "warmed up", "in" sin. The environments that will shape us have already been shaped by humanity's rebellion and rejection of the Father's plans and purpose. We are knitted together (literally "twisted") physically and emotionally in a sin-broken environment. The traumatic and potentially misshaping nature of our formation is doubly evident in the Hebrew version of this verse, because the word for "iniquities" is based on a root that means "to distort", "to twist" or "to pervert" as well.

If a child is born with a physical deformity it is easy to see the misshaping effects of sin in their formation. But increasingly psychologists are discovering how the stresses, fears and abuse experienced by an expectant mother leave their mark on the psyche of the unborn child.[29] We enter life already mortally wounded.

As a young adult and an expectant father I was praying one day when I had a picture of myself watching the world from behind a window. In my picture I knew I was safe, but the world was muted, though I didn't realise this because for me this was my "normal".

I cooperated with the Spirit. I simply asked Jesus to break the glass barrier, so that I could better engage with the world, to feel its breezes, smell its smells and better hear its sounds. Nothing happened at the time, but the day my first child was born a rush of multi-coloured emotions hit me like I'd never felt them before.

Over the years I've changed, layer-by-layer, sometimes in experiences like the one above and other times imperceptibly. Active permission and response are ways in which we cooperate with the Spirit's work in us.

I'm still not the world's most effusive person and people hug me deliberately because they know I'm not a spontaneous hugger. Outwardly, I still carry a scar from my formative experiences. But I feel the world with new passions. A sunset can move me; children and babies can make me cry with wonder.

These are little steps in our story and testimonies to the victory of Jesus in us. Jesus' victory in us has not taken away our history. He has redeemed it; given it new value; grown bigger victories in the fields of our defeats and pain; turned our scars into the stories that make us unique.

Jesus is such a good Redeemer. He turns something ugly into something beautiful in a new setting. Jesus doesn't plan the death and sorrow into which we are born, but He plans for it. He transforms it so that our scars not only tell our story, they point to His story and they make us more fearful to the devil who gave us the scars in the first place.

Jesus carries the ugly scar of the cross into eternity and yet, what was ugly when it happened has become the most beautiful idea ever thought and the greatest story ever told. Everything can be beautiful in its time and in its setting, when connected to heaven through the blood of the Lamb.

So my own struggles seem to have left some positive consequences in me too. In particular, I have a lot of faith and authority in life-threatening situations, particularly in hospitals and medical centres. In fact, most of my favourite miracle stories have a hospital in them somewhere. There was Rebecca whose car-smashed body would never walk again; Phil, raised from the dead; and of course Liz whose story I told above. They all happened in hospitals.

The battle over our destiny starts as we are being wonderfully woven together. Sin seeks to entangle, frustrate and own us at every point that would write our life-story in order to stop us becoming the producer-maker-builder we were made to become.

Raising Cain

Now Cain's story has more to it than is immediately obvious.

In Genesis the devil is presented as personified sin, like a hungry animal craving Cain (see Genesis 4:7). The devil is a devourer of souls,[30] greedy for people's inner-lives. The devil's destructive relationship with mankind is not just fuelled by his desire to hurt God and to be a god himself; it is far more chaotic than that.

You see, like us, the devil is a son of God (Job 1:6) who has rejected his Father's plans and purposes for him. He was an angel, Lucifer. His name meant "bringer of light"[31] and light was God's first gift to creation (Genesis 1:3). Lucifer had a calling and a resource: he was to bring light to the world. Instead he slithered into the shadows and told lies.

When we reject our calling we actually deny the value in us, because God calls us in line with the essence and image we carry, the hallmarks that prove our value.

By rejecting his calling to bring light, the devil denied his own value and this angelic bringer of shining light became a hoarder of other people's glory. Like Smaug, the dragon in Tolkien's *The Hobbit*, the devil can only know value from the pile of gold he sits on top of.

The human soul carries an aftertaste of the divine nature, a gust of God's breath (Genesis 2:7). The devil, cut off from the intimacy with the God he was made for, will suck up this precious distillate wherever he can find it. Access to the human soul gives him access to the taste of heaven, without having to come into God's presence.

The devil is an addict craving the affection and submission of our hearts; comfort-eating his way through the value the Father invested into every human life.

As with Cain's parents before him, the devil won Cain's life by telling a lie. But this time the job was so much easier, because Cain had been born in pain with an inclination towards offence.

When God approved of Abel's offering He was not making a value judgement on either brother or on the attitude in which they made their offerings.[32] God was working to a heavenly plan that neither Cain nor Abel could see from their perspective, under the sun. In approving Abel's offering, the Father was endorsing the idea of blood sacrifice as the model that would explain His redemptive actions in Christ. But the inclination towards pain in Cain made him feel God's approval of his brother competitively: it was a criticism, a value judgement on Cain too. Jealous for approval, Cain killed his competition.

Strangely, Cain's actions amplified the meaning and value of Abel's testimony; and while they reduced Cain's they didn't destroy it altogether.

Abel became a bigger picture of the cross than his animal offering alone. He became the first righteous man to die for sins that were not his (Matthew 23:35). And in a beautiful, prophetic irony his offering, a sacrifice from his livestock, became the "mark" of grace, put by God onto Cain; one that saved him from the consequences of his sin (Genesis 4:15). That "mark" became a sign of the covenant and ... it revealed Jesus. Let me explain:

The Hebrew word used for Cain's "mark" is the same word used for the "sign" of the covenant later in the Bible. It is made up of three Hebrew letters: aleph, yod and tav. When the Bible was first written down, Hebrew letters didn't look the way they do today. Each letter was a pictogram. The aleph pictogram was a bull's head, the biggest animal you could sacrifice and which Abel had given from his herds. Two crossed sticks represented the third letter Tav and Abel would have sacrificed his offering on a criss-cross of burning sticks. But the middle letter, the yod, pointed to a sacrifice bigger that Abel's: it was drawn as a stake, a tent peg or a nail.

The sign of grace written onto Cain was a picture of the biggest sacrifice nailed to a wooden cross.

Even as a victim, Abel's rightness before God turned the evil done to him into a testimony. When we find forgiveness for those who have abused and hurt us, the cross grows in us and even our pain connects to the goodness of God. The scars we carry, in body, in mind or in spirit, become the chapter headings in our life story, whether we want them to or not, but their meaning isn't fixed until life's final full-stop – which is why we should leave no location to the devil.

I suspect that Cain should have been Jesus' ancestor. I say that because when Cain was born, Eve says of him, "I have gotten a man *with* God" (Genesis 4:1). The word translated "with" is normally left un-translated in English Bibles because it just plays a grammatical role. In this sentence it sort of joins the words "man" and "God". Cain is literally a Man-God. He is not *the* Man-God, but I suspect Eve saw him as part of the "seed" promised to her in the previous chapter (Genesis 3:15).

Now that little word "with" is actually a contracted form of that word for Cain's "mark". It is made up of just the first and last letters of the word for Cain's "mark", aleph and tav. Or in pictograms, a bull on a cross. These two letters also happen to be the first and last letters of the Hebrew alphabet, the Old Testament version of the alpha and omega, the symbol of Jesus.

Cain should have been in the line of the Man-God, the ultimate sacrifice, who would be bruised, crushing the serpent's head. Instead Cain took on the serpent's way of thinking, becoming an addict to other people's glory. He lost this first calling and became an unproductive wanderer (Genesis 4:12).

But Jesus still redeemed something from Cain's crime. Cain is the first man saved under the sign of the cross. Cain still pointed to Jesus, just not as a forbear. He was one of the many who didn't walk in his calling in this life, but that didn't mean he wasn't saved. Nor did it mean that his Father couldn't redeem purpose from his life.

As life unfolds for each of us, the world's imperfections mean we experience disappointment and injustice alongside incredible provision and blessing. In our early years our psyches will develop to deal with the pains and losses we were not designed for. We learn to self-protect to safeguard our wounds; and to self-promote to compensate for the value that's been taken from us.

Taking opportunity through our God-like sensitivity to pain over sin, sin sucks the sense of value out of us and writes a story based on a self-perpetuating cycle of wounds and wants in the heart. In some areas we become over-sensitive and in others over-bearing and, unbalanced, we run races that make sense under the sun, but not under heaven.

But even when sin has done its worst, it is still possible to see the God-shaped purpose in a life and, as with Abel, it often seems that the more someone has lost, the more the Lord uses what He salvages.

Sins of the Father

Just last week I went to speak in a town in the east of England that I had not been to before. The night before I went, I felt the Lord say that there would be someone in the meeting who had just recently been stabbed. So when I got up to speak I mentioned this! There was total silence from the congregation; no one responded. After I had spoken I was praying for people who were queuing up for prophetic prayer and healing when suddenly there was a man in front of me.

I recognised him; he had walked out of the meeting shortly after I had shared how Jesus had healed me from cancer as a teenager.

As I looked at him he put his hands up defensively and said, "I'm not a Christian, I just brought my mum tonight and she said I had to come and talk to you because of what you said about someone who was stabbed recently."

He went on to explain that he had been stabbed the previous week protecting his little brother. I felt I should tell him that Jesus had looked after him since he had been a small boy in the same way that he had looked after his brother. This obviously meant something to him. He explained that when he had been stabbed he would probably have been killed, but the knife had caught on his leather belt, so God had looked after him. He had also had a violent father and had often protected his younger brother from his father,

61

but there had been no one to protect him back then.

Then out of the blue he said to me, "Is your sister called Debbie?" I said, "Yes." I have a sister who is eleven years younger than me called Debbie. Then he said, "I know about you, she told me about you getting healed from cancer when we were in school. I've known about you all my life!"

The impact of what Jesus had arranged that night only really hit me in the days that followed. I checked with my sister who remembered John. He had been around when I was away from home at University. He had come to various youth events before he had moved away from London to escape his violent father and start a new life. This was when his mother had become a Christian. Jesus had impacted John in the past. On this night John had driven his mum to a meeting and stayed long enough to hear someone he didn't know give a word of knowledge that related to his present life and then tell a story that reminded him of a past in which he had known a God who had loved him and protected him; who was still protecting him now.

The dots were joining up ... John acknowledged that God was looking after him. It was still difficult for him to see God as Father, but John could now at least see how God was like a protective older brother. Apparently, John's mum had told him the same things in the past. But the coincidences of that Saturday night meant it was harder not to see and to feel its truth.

Most of us haven't experienced a home life like John's. But the struggles of our early lives always seek to separate us from the provision and love of our Father God. The frustrations of work keep even good Fathers away from the home, creating wants in the heart. And even when they are present, their own damage can often hurt even their best loved children, leaving wounds to be protected from further injury.

It's easy to understand our parents as we become adults, so we forgive them for missing birthdays and not letting us gorge ourselves on chocolate all day. But by the time we understand our disappointments we have already been shaped by them.

Salvation is not just about going to heaven, it is about the change in the deepest parts of who we are to demonstrate heaven's purpose even in life's chaos.

Overcomers see the testimony written in their history. Father was ordering events in your life according to His plans while respecting your freedoms. He is drawing you towards the future that He has always wanted you to discover.

The real you and the race you were made to run will emerge by revelation not information. But as we saw with Peter, information can become revelation as we process it with Jesus, so I want you to start collecting information about your life.

"Write the vision down, and inscribe it on stone, that the one who reads it can run." (Habakkuk 2:2)

There is a race to be run and your story so far can become the vision that inspires you to run it. So I'm going to ask you to write your story as you see it now, under the sun; and expect Jesus to give you His perspective: the same story, but now under heaven.

At the end of the last chapter you mapped out the stages of your life story so far. Now we're going to fill in the steps, starting with your birth and early years. To help in the process I will tell you some of my story too.

Our Childhood's Pattern

My parents lived by their faith in Jesus. I was born into a home that was open to anyone that needed a bed. In the days before bureaucracy killed this type of kindness the police would drop off an assortment of vagrants, the desperate and the mentally and spiritually troubled.

At the same time, my father used to smuggle Bibles into the old Communist Bloc countries of Eastern Europe, visiting and supporting underground churches and Bible schools. We spent a lot of time in continental Europe travelling from place to place in a VW camper van. The contrasts and colours of the pre-school period of my life were so different from the ones that followed in a more settled London suburb that my memories of them haven't been lost among the more regular experiences of later childhood.

In Yugoslavia I was fascinated by a pig that was shoving its snout through the rough slats of its pen. Thinking it would be fun to go into the pen with the pigs I unlatched the gate, only to be rudely shoved aside by a delighted sow squeaking oinks of liberty as she led her fattening offspring to a future free of barbecues and apple sauce. I ran back to our Dormobile in tears, ashamed and too scared to tell my parents what I had done. The pigs made the most of their free-range status, requiring half the village to round them up. My concerned parents concluded wrongly that I had been chased and scared by the herd. I gladly concurred with their perspective. You learn at a young age that looking like a victim can help you avoid responsibility and a white lie covers a multitude of shames. I was in my thirties before I came clean.

More seriously, in this former communist state a truck knocked me down as I ran across the road. Its bumper hit me on the head and threw me some distance. This was my second brush with death. I don't remember the impact, but I do remember looking at the feet of the crowd that surrounded me and I remember the feeling of the pulling thread as they stitched up my head under local anaesthetic in a featureless hospital that looked more like a swimming pool changing room. My face was covered with a cloth and I remember my mother lifting the edge to look in and give me reassuring eye contact. To this day I have an enormous scar and a dent in my skull, which I assume means that a piece of my head must have been left in the region.

Unfortunately, all this rich experience did not equip me in the slightest for the shock of a regular UK primary school. My first few years of formal education were a bit of a disaster. The school I went to adopted some new "cutting edge" approaches to education. Ones that didn't believe in structure or discipline. We had a wild time. So much so that a more experienced lady was drafted in to help my regular, but newly qualified teacher. Forty years later and in a different town we would meet again and realise our shared history as she re-found a faith she had lost when her marriage broke down.

My parents expressed their concern to this first school that at nearly six years old I wasn't able read. The school didn't deem this to be their problem, but they did send me off to be tested for dyslexia, which I didn't have.

My schooling wasn't helped by the fact that as a family we still travelled extensively. With a lack of English-speaking playmates, my first sister and I learnt to amuse ourselves. My parents bought me two decks of playing cards in Norway. The students my parents were teaching taught me a host of card games and conjuring-tricks. I spent hours thinking about the ways patterns allowed you to predict the likelihoods and outcomes of various card hands.

When I wasn't playing with my cards I would sometimes sit in on my father's teaching, trying to understand what he was talking about. Something must have gone in because today I am constantly surprised by my own biblical knowledge! During our travels I got to be known by an American missionary couple to Europe. At two points in my future this couple was to play a key role in opening up opportunities for me.

As I hit seven years old my parents planted a church, moved and set up a more settled home. This was my first brush with church planting, a practice that has been a constant thread through my adult life. My parents finally succeeded in getting me into a new school.

My new school was a total shock for me. In Europe, being the English-speaking children had often made my sister and me the centre of attention. But now in school I was different for all the wrong reasons. The other children had known each other for three years already. What I thought made me special was not valued at all. I didn't know the rules of football, nor the teams I should support. I didn't know how to establish myself verbally. My father continued to travel a lot, but we couldn't travel with him. I started to resent his absences.

Another boy, Mark, started at this school the same week that I did. He lived round the corner and we became friends. I saw Mark last month for the first time in years. He pointed out what a huge influence being my friend had had on him. He became a Christian and met his wife through the church we went to as teenagers.

Life took on a strange duality. In school I was a nervous outsider, in church a cocky dominator. I was learning how to develop different personas for different contexts.

In my desire to fit in at my new school I became naughty and lazy, so much so that I was tested to see if I was ESN (Educationally Sub-Normal). The results showed I was simply lazy. But a pattern was emerging and I was labelling myself: I was a late reader; I needed special testing at both of my primary schools; I frustrated my teachers. I concluded I was stupid.

At eleven we would all take the 11+ exam. The Grammar Schools had been closed, but the standard test remained for a while. It would show that I had the highest IQ in the school, which shocked me. It also triggered a process in me that helped me climb out of the box I had been put in. Over the years my complicated relationship with academic achievement and qualifications has been a defining source of value and identity to me, both positively and negatively.

But that is in the future. At primary school, naughtiness gave me some level of popularity, particularly with others who, for various reasons, felt excluded from the mainstream. My naughtiness led me to being one of only two children ever to be caned at my primary school.[33] It may have been painful, but it also made me different from my peers and being different made me feel very special too!

I started to develop a subversively insouciant attitude towards authority.

As I look back on my early years I can see the connection between the events and experiences that moulded me and my character and behaviours. I see the attacks of the enemy: both the outright ones, my brushes with death, and the subtler ones, such as his attempts to shape my attitudes and beliefs towards my gifts and education. But I also see the hand of God: in the acquaintances I made and in the lessons I was absorbing, and in the strengths He put into my character. I can see the roots of the things that enable me, motivate me and relax me ... the things that make me "me".

Your Story

Now it's your turn. I've been brief in my story above, but if you can, write a fuller account of your own life. I know my story and don't want to bore you with more detail than is necessary. But Jesus died to give our lives eternal meaning and He wants us to value what He has valued. The more moments you can capture the better. Jesus wants to share each one with you. Although they have passed, they live on in who you are.

Ask Him to be with you in the process and to bring things to mind.

Now note down:

What do you know about your birth? Were you planned or a surprise? Did your parents have any particular hopes or aspirations for you?

What are your earliest memories? What are the incidents that most define your early years? Did you feel happy or sad at these times?

Have you faced any traumas or life or death situations? Where was Jesus when you did?

If there are real injustices in your past, recognise them as such. Reject these locations as being part of God's plan for you, but ask

Jesus to show you how His plans have anticipated and provided a contingency for these works of the enemy.

How far back does your memory go?

If it doesn't go back very far, ask Jesus to show you why. You may not get an instant answer, but my experience is that this is a question He will not ignore – though He may take time in answering it. We need to be ready for what He shows us.

Can you see any connections emerging between your early memories and later behaviour? What were your battles? What were your successes? Who were your influencers? Are there attitudes and views you hold today that root back to your early experiences? And if so, do those experiences feel like they belong to Jesus or to the devil?

Make a note of the impressions and memories that come back to you in this process. It is useful if you can make these notes somewhere that you will not lose easily, so they can be added to and reviewed as you work through this book.

Don't rush on now. Take time on this dialogue.

Endnotes

26. Hebrew *t'shuwqah* is a strong word that conveys yearning, deep desire or lust.

27. The Hebrew word "chuwl" used here is translated "shapen" in the King James Bible, but it properly means to "twist" or "whirl" and can be used negatively. It is often used of the twisting of a mother in childbirth, but the connection to "iniquity" in this verse meant the sense of twisting out of shape seemed appropriate. Because the word for "iniquity" used here also has its root in a word meaning to bend, twist or distort.

28. The Hebrew word "yacham" means literally to warm or make hot. It is sometimes translated "conceived", but the full gestation period is probably the process in view, not just the moment of conception.

29. Researchers are discovering that our construction during pregnancy is actually a better indicator of certain problems in later life than our DNA. The Barker Theory, as it is now called, proposes a model of human life similar to the relationship between the architect (the DNA) and the construction contractor

(the womb/placenta). The design might be perfect, but cheap material and poor workmanship is ultimately more important to the quality of the house being built. Emotions, activity, diet and environment can all effect development in the womb.

30. The image of the "devourer of Souls" is used by Ezekiel (see 22:25) to describe the false prophets, but Ezekiel tends to prophesy to the spiritual reality behind a person or people (see chapter 28 and his prophecy to the the King of Tyre who is also the fallen angel of Eden). And so Peter picks up this image from Ezekiel and applies it to the devil in 1 Peter 5:8.

31. This is the literal meaning of the Septuagint rendering "heōsphoros" of the Hebrew word/name "hêlēl".

32. It is often taught that Cain didn't bring his best, whereas Abel did. But I can find no evidence in the text to justify this assertion. I think it is made to explain God's response, but the explanation given above for God's approval of an offering of blood is far stronger, particularly when you see the development in the Pentateuch of the theological understanding put into the sacrificed lamb.

33. While rare in the 1970's, schools were still allowed to use a good spanking to instill moral fibre.

CHAPTER 4

SOLVING A STRANGE CASE OF

MISSHAPEN IDENTITY

"The Lord your God will bless you in all your increase, and in all the work of your hands, and you shall be altogether joyful." (Deuteronomy 16:15)

Work is not a product of the fall, frustration in our work is!

In the Beginning:

"...God blessed them and said to them: 'Be fruitful and multiply, fill up the earth and subdue it, have dominion.'" (Genesis 1:28a)

This was God's first commission; a calling true for all humanity that made sense of the name God had given them, "Adam". We are all supposed to be productive with the world and to make it work for us.

Every time God judged creation to be "good" (Genesis 1:4,10,12 etc.), He affirmed its essential value because the Hebrew word for "good" also means "valuable". But after He had made and then commissioned men and women, the Bible tells us:

"God approved what He had made, it was all very valuable." (Genesis 1:31a)

As a producer-maker-builder, mankind added value to creation, simply by being a part of it.

Producing is about releasing the potential already in the things around us. A producer gets apples from apple trees. Making goes further, it gives new potential to the things we have already; we make boxes, tables and chairs from trees that ordinarily make apples and acorns. And building takes our making beyond ourselves. It's our "fruit that remains". We build farms with orchards of apple trees; homes of wood and stone that we can pass on to the families we raise in them.

There is something about being a builder that completes the fruitfulness in us. It is what we build that outlasts us and leaves a legacy beyond death, which is the subject on which this book will end.

Jesus, a real-life builder, didn't just ply this trade for the twenty-odd years of adult life; He was a builder in creation too. It is Jesus speaking in the Old Testament when it says:

"Before His works of old, from everlasting *I was anointed...* I was beside Him as *a master builder*." (Proverbs 22b-23a, 30a)

Being a builder in life was more than just a day job for Jesus, it was Jesus being on earth what He was in heaven.

Peter, having met the risen Jesus, goes fishing (John 21:1-2), which tells me that fishing was more than just a career option for Peter. I suspect throwing out the net was in his blood physically and evangelistically. And being a tentmaker seems to capture something of the traveller Paul.

Jesus, Peter and Paul all went beyond their natural calling when the glory descended on them. But none of them ever lost the careers that made them who they were.

There are works for us to walk in, prepared beforehand by a Father who knows us better than we know ourselves.

Whether as a carer, administrator, writer, sports coach, accountant, teacher or civic leader, we are all made to be producer-maker-builders, metaphorically if not literally, adding more value to the world than we take from it. That's the theory. But if we all did what we knew we should do, we'd all be healthy, wealthy and skinny – and some might question whether I'm any of those. But there are areas of life in which I now know I'm fruitful and add value.

Rebel Without a Cause

At the age of eleven I didn't feel particularly valuable. I was a disappointment to my parents, uncovered as a thief and a liar. I was a frustration to my teachers, educationally sub-normal and a slow reader. To my peers I was the un-sporty kid who went to church. But deep inside me there was a determination to be "something". It was just that I didn't know what thing.

I found an identity on the edge of the crowd, far enough from the centre to be different, but close enough not to feel rejected by the majority.

The only fact that didn't fit my assessment of myself was my coming top in the "Eleven Plus" exam. The results had been read in reverse order. It started to dawn on me that my name hadn't been called, so I assumed I was due for a special private chat with my headmaster. My paper must have been so bad they hadn't given me a score. When my name was eventually read out I was too surprised to really enjoy the moment. Well-meaning friends expressed congratulations on my getting lucky.

But that year I passed another exam which won me a place at a selective school. My primary school headmaster had advised my parents they were wasting their time and money. The school they wanted to send me to, while not expensive, still cost money they didn't have. Which is when the American missionaries, Fred and Sharon Wright, stepped in. Unbeknown to me, they helped to pay my fees.

The maths paper of the entrance exam proved to be one of those turning points in life, a step directed by the Lord that goes beyond human planning (Proverbs 16:9). As I stared blankly at the questions in front of me I felt a rising anxiety; I was going to disappoint my parents again. So I did something different: I prayed. Light came and the questions made sense. I was given a place at the school because my maths was so strong.

My new school would be very different from my two previous schools, not letting me drift lazily. The headmaster, Derek Fenner, saw more in me than I saw in myself. Even when I burnt a part of my school down he was wistfully hopeful for me, rather than damningly caustic.

In time, the school gave me a desire to learn and stretch myself academically. But in my first few years I simply adopted the patterns I had established at my previous schools.

I found a comfortable place among the mild misfits in the bottom streams, often in trouble but not really destructive or unkind.

But as I got older the trouble got worse. I had to go to greater extremes to feel the thrill and kudos of misadventure. I fell in with the "scum of the earth" as my history teacher told my parents.

It had started off with mild misdemeanours. We, my scummy friends and I, would break into a local cinema, by way of a broken window and an unguarded fire exit, to watch films without payment or censorship.

Soon we were stealing chemicals from the school labs. Hydrochloric acid to melt things and various explosive chemicals. One experiment almost ended disastrously. I had been persuaded to hide a fist full of sodium in my lunchbox. We had seen how sodium exploded in water and our chemistry teacher had remarked it was far more impressive in acid, but that was too dangerous for school.

Somehow I managed to get the sodium to Streatham Station without it destroying my school bag. We bought a cheap lemon drink as our acid. I was to drop the sodium into the drink, but in my nervousness I dropped the cup. With no more money for supplies, a bolder friend, Warren, went behind a tree and refilled the cup the way nature intended. The ensuing explosion was impressive and the timing immaculate as a train pulled in and a hundred commuters disembarked to a shower of burning rain. Warren had to go to hospital with burns to his hand.

But then there was an occasion that shook me up. We had been riding a train without tickets. The carriage was empty and two of the group had seriously vandalised the carriage. They urinated, slashed seats and threw light bulbs at cars as we crossed bridges. I went home disturbed.

I knew something had to change. Life seemed to be running out of control and I was only fourteen.

A Freudian Slip

At the start of the 20th century the great-grandfather of modern psychology, Sigmund Freud, observed that mankind had two primal drives. We commonly call these two drives: sex and aggression.

You need some sex if you're going to fill up the earth and you need something like aggression if you are going to subdue it. So to be honest, Freud's great contribution to human understanding has been on page one of the Bible for millennia.

Anyway, these two powerful motivators fill the gap between the image of God in us and the commission of God on us. He has made us producer-maker-builders and commissioned us to fill up and subdue the Earth, and judged us as very valuable.

But in a fallen and frustrated world the God-given tri-part blessing of Value, Fruitfulness and Authority, has become the three-stranded curse of Money, Sex and Power.

Something has become twisted in our desires. But the problem goes deeper than just our motivations. It goes to the source of our identity.

Even political thinker and atheist Karl Marx recognised that man added value to the world; that he was distinct from other animals by virtue of being a producer.[34]

So it's interesting that we now live in a society that defines us as consumers. By what we take from the world, rather than what we put into it – the things, wealth, people and positions we collect to ourselves; the money, sex and power we accumulate – rather than the life beyond us that we release and resource by our value, fruitfulness and authority.

Of course, mankind has always had to consume, but consuming was a function of life not an expression of it. Consuming can be good and pleasurable, but it is not the foundation of our identity and worth, nor is it the hope of our calling.

Adam was fruitful enough that he didn't need to eat everything he grew. The fruit from the tree in the middle of the Garden was supposed to be given back to the Lord (Genesis 2:16-17).

Adam and Eve ate that fruit. They redefined themselves according to a desire (Genesis 3:6); as consumers of fruit rather than as fruitful producers.

Desires that should have moved them to make, ended up driving them to take.

Under heaven, the desires in you will motivate you in your calling. But disconnected from Father's purposes and plans, desires can become destructive urges, pointless lusts, hungers, needs that propel us forward. The engine is running and the clutch is engaged, but without a destination or hands on the wheel, life is an accident waiting to happen at the first bend in the road.

Desire without direction will take you on a very random journey, creating a haphazard life story as you bounce between whatever scratches the itch or feeds the hunger. But the desires themselves are not wrong or bad; they were a gift to you to motivate you into discovering who God made you to be. Which means embracing the motives in you, while at the same time realising that they probably need some untangling and attaching to a heavenly purpose.

The image in us gets twisted by sin, misshaped just enough to shift our sense of identity towards the things we've collected, owned and consumed, rather than what we add to the world. The shift is subtle, but profound. We will feel wants when in fact we have enough and we will be wounded by those who suck up our value to feed their own needs.

A third great thinker of the twentieth century, Albert Einstein once said:

"Strive not for success, but rather to be of value." I suspect he was right about the $E=mc^2$ stuff, and Albert's onto something when he says we should be of value. But he needs to lose the striving.

It is the wounds and wants of the heart that mean we strive for success to feel value.

Success is not the same as fruit. When people encounter your fruit it can build them up, but when they encounter your success it tends to leave them feeling a little bit smaller.

And when we strive after anything, even a good thing, we'll often find the target of our desires has actually become the success of endeavour, over and above the noble cause we started out to pursue.

Now we're made to achieve great things, but life is a gift to be used to add value to the world, not a competition to win at any cost.

Most of the world will find a misshapen identity in their sexual and aggressive appetites and achievements. "Who have I married/bedded?"; "Am I gay or straight?"; "Have I got it?" and if not, "Can I get it?"; "What bits of my/your life are under my control?" Like the writer of Ecclesiastes, many will eventually recognise that an excess of sexual and civic achievements are not the route to a satisfied life (Ecclesiastes 2:1-11). But many will still die trying.

En route we build personas to cover the person, images of ourselves to be entertained in our imaginations and pursued in our actions. Based on our felt need for glory rather than the glory already in us, on a sense of lack rather than on knowledge of worth, we act out our distorted images grabbing glory from the wrong places, exploiting our talents and uniqueness rather than enjoying them.

Under the sun there are no other options. But under heaven there is a plan:

To solve the strange case of our misshapen identity.

The first phase of that plan, as we saw with Jesus, involves the discovery of the fruitful you.

Paul tells us to: "grow up in all things into Him" (Ephesians 4:15). It is the growth of what we already have that defines us, not the acquiring of what we think we need.

It's the meek who inherit the earth, not the determined.

As a builder, Jesus had experienced "favour with God and with men" (Luke 2:59). He demonstrated the blessing promised in Deuteronomy 16:15 at the beginning of this chapter.

Today Judith and I live in Cookham, a village on the edge of Maidenhead by the Thames. It's a beautiful part of the world; a place where people aspire to live, but we got to live here by accident. I say accident, but really I mean we were called here. We are here by favour, not by any goal, plan or provision we made. What we did do was cooperate with the Father's promptings and patternings.

God prompted, we stepped out in faith and He opened the doors and led me into a career in IT I hadn't expected or even wanted.

Back in 1995 I was living and working in inner city London. I had grown up there and expected to serve Jesus my whole life there. I led a church-planting ministry that had literally gone global. But we "lived by faith", which is a way of saying that I was doing Christian ministry without receiving enough money to live on. We saw some wonderful provisions, but finances were a real strain and credit card debts were creeping up on us. To make matters worse, we owned a small flat, but the value of housing had crashed in the UK just as we bought it. We owed more than we owned.

Then on January 2nd 1996 I was given a prophetic word from someone I didn't know. Six weeks later Judith and I found ourselves living in a new town and I was working in an IT role that I wasn't qualified for; that experienced programmers would have sold a kidney to get onto their CVs.

My new employer more than doubled our income. He even rented a house for us and paid our relocation costs for eight months. Fifteen years later he would contact me over Christmas to ask me to pray for the dying wife of one of his salesmen, but I've already told you that story.

From 1996 to 2003 I would help to grow a software company from three to over thirty employees and associates. We joined a church, which I would end up leading. We cleared our debts and were able to buy a house. The hand of The Lord was so clearly in the move from London. But for the first few years I was in real confusion.

You see, I had felt called to ministry ever since my healing from cancer aged sixteen. Yet here I was in a secular vocation that Jesus had clearly led me into, experiencing obvious favour with God and men.

Looking back, I can see Father's grace, provision and encouragement on my logical and problem solving skills. A career in IT and business solutions was not necessarily the only way to be faithful with these natural gifts, but it was a valid expression for them. Despite the obvious favour on these skills I had consistently under-valued them.

But every gift and desire given to us has a unique ability to shape and teach us.

In my enthusiasm I had rushed into a ministry in which I would use my technical skills, but would never be stretched in them or by them. But now, in the market place I learnt about multi-million pound projects, how to manage risk, project plan, budgeting and cost control. I was paid a good salary to solve logic problems. It did my sense of value no end of good too.

I hadn't realised how my sense of self-worth had been worn down in a ministry where I continually lived on a shoestring. When Jesus said, "love your neighbour" He added "as you love yourself" (Matthew 19:19b). If you don't value yourself then giving yourself to your neighbour doesn't impart any value to them either.

Actually, my sense of self worth wasn't that high when I had gone into ministry in the first place. For years I'd been striving for value through a worthy cause, rather than expressing the value in me.

The Lord is not ultimately looking for servants to do His bidding, He is raising sons and daughters who will walk in their value and authority to administer His work with Him. Faithfulness with the natural value in us releases eternal riches and it is by stretching us that Father reveals our real shape.

An Unusual Patterning of Events

While we need to solve our case of misshapen identity *for* ourselves, we don't have to solve it *by* ourselves. As we saw in *The Supra-Natural Life*, it is the major task of the Holy Spirit in us to search our hearts and transform us according to the image of His Son (Romans 8:26-29).

The Spirit works in us often at a subconscious level, but the Father has also been providing people and experiences for us throughout our lives; events that untangle and encourage us in the ways we should go.

One of God's covenant names in the Old Testament is "the LORD Provides" or "the LORD sees". "Pro-vision" is literally "fore-seeing", so "providence" is "the foreseeing care and guidance of God".[35] Providence is a gift that nudges and draws us through the days Father has thought about for us.

Father God will providentially supply experiences, people and gifts in one season that can ready us for and direct us towards a future beyond our human horizons.

Providence is often easier to see with hindsight than it is in the moment. And with the Holy Spirit's help it is possible to discern the patterns in our pasts that point to the Father's hope for our future. Seeing Father's providence in our history will release a sense of our value that's not based on performing, but on knowing that the eyes and thoughts of the Father are turned towards His child. It will also give us a greater confidence in our calling, not based on self-promoting pride, but on submitted obedience.

You may not see it right now, but I can guarantee that you'll find evidence of the Father's plans for your life in your past if you take the time to look for it.

In the early 1990s I came across some research by the "Alister Hardy Religious Experience Research Centre".[36] They collected and analysed people's religious experiences. Their research showed that over two thirds of people in the Western world would claim to have had a "religious" experience, the most common type being what researchers called an "unusual patterning of events".

By this they meant that coincidences started to stack up in ways that caught a person's attention and led to an experience of God's love or of a presence watching over them. About one third of cynical, rational Westerners have seen the providence of God in their lives without even looking for it. So I know that if you seek it, you'll find it.

These unusual patterns are the evidence of God's plans for us; they are not in themselves the steps and stages of it. They are also one of the most common ways the Lord speaks to us – the fingerprints of a good God in our misshapen history. As we see the patterns, the disjointed moments of our lives start to get joined up, one mini-pattern joins to another mini-pattern and a picture starts to emerge.

Now we hit a bit of a chicken and egg situation. The clearer we see who we are made to be, the easier it is to see the provision of God in our stories. But at the same time, it is seeing the unusual patterns that can help us solve the mystery of our misshapen identity. The more untangled our desires and motives are, the more we'll find life lines up with the hope of calling. At the same time, it is that hope that draws us forward in a way that changes us.

We'll look at how His Father's provision pointed to Jesus' vocational calling and I'll show you some of what I've seen in my own story. But what really matters is that you see the Father's thoughts over you and your life.

Jesus the builder

At the age when I was breaking into cinemas and stealing sodium, i.e. thirteen or fourteen, Jesus entered the adult world. He became fruitful with His natural gifts by becoming a builder. It is part of the transition into maturity that we start producing more than we consume. To do that means we have to start being something, which means we can no longer be anything we want to be.

I'm not suggesting you'll fully know your professional calling in your teens, but it is the natural age to start adding value to the world with the gifts in you. Be faithful with what you've got because "to him who has, more is given" (Mark 4:25).

As a builder Jesus was being faithful in the three ways we thought about in the first chapter of this book: in the little things; with wealth or mammon; and with the things that belonged to someone else. Seeing how His faith worked with His Father's plans will help us exercise faith on our journey too.

From eternity to here

Mark's Gospel starts Jesus' story at the Jordan. He reminds us that whatever has gone before is irrelevant compared with the eternity ahead of us. But the other three Gospels all start their accounts of

Jesus from a perspective that highlights the role of history, friends, family and even eternity in preparing and shaping Jesus.

Luke starts his account with Jesus' extended family, with Mary and her cousins. Matthew starts his account in Israel's history with Israel's founders and kings; Abraham through David to Joseph and Jesus. John starts his account in the eternity behind us: "In the beginning was the Word."

Though we may not be able to see it, every life shares these perspectives: where it's heading, family, history and the plans of heaven.

Jesus was born into a family that loved Him to the best of its ability. It wasn't perfect, but it had some understanding of its spiritual inheritance and conveyed that to Jesus. Some families are better at this than others, but all families carry positive spiritual and natural promises whether they realise it or not. And we can stand in the benefits of that inheritance by how we relate to our parents, both naturally and spiritually.

Jesus had both a natural and a spiritual parent. He was born of Mary, but adopted by Joseph. Despite not being a physical heir, Jesus still received the rights to David's throne through Joseph, because faith trumps genetics every time.

"So know that those who are of faith, these are Abraham's children ... So those of faith are blessed with the faithful Abraham." (Galatians 3:7-9)

Joseph's acceptance of Jesus as his son by faith and Jesus' honouring of Joseph as His father by faith, brought Jesus into Joseph's kingly line, while Mary gave Jesus the genetic link that made sense of the promises made to David's offspring.

We all have both natural and spiritual parents. It would be easy to imagine that parents are only a provision if they are obviously spiritual and kind. But actually, even bad parents and adoptive parents can connect you to the purposes of heaven.

Part of my problem at age thirteen was that while I loved my parents, I had to pay an emotional price for their radical life choices. Today, as an adult, I understand their choices intellectually, but I experienced them and they shaped me emotionally as child. The cost left an unfocussed, quiet anger hidden in the dark recesses of my soul – one that resented my inheritance from them. If anyone ever asked I would say that I believed in God, but was never going to do "Christian work".

But Moses tells us:

"I, the LORD God, am a zealous God, visiting the iniquities of the fathers on the children, to the third and fourth generation of those who hate me; but showing kind favour to the thousandth of those who love me and keep my commands." (Deuteronomy 5:9-10)

The word "visiting" can mean "paying attention to". God doesn't punish children for the sins of their parents (Ezekiel 18:20), this verse is simply saying that God pays attention to the effects sin will have in our children and those around us too.

But if we can overcome the offence caused by our parent's failings there is a far bigger blessing to walk in. Twisting sin can affect three or four generations, but blessings can have an affect through a thousand generations if the recipient loves God.

A thousand generations connects us to the full sweep of covenant history and people. I suspect every life on earth has a good spiritual inheritance in their family line, even if it's too far back for us to be conscious of it. Jesus didn't need to understand every aspect of His spiritual roots in order to draw on their benefits. An attitude of honour towards His parents and submission to His Heavenly Father's providence bought Him into an alignment with more promises and blessings than Jesus could have worked out what to do with.

Family Business

When Jesus was four years old, Joseph moved the family back to Nazareth. The reasons were very practical. About three miles north of Nazareth lay the town of Sepphoris, the new capital city of Galilee. From around 3 BC and through most of Jesus' life Sepphoris was one of the ancient world's biggest building projects.

While not specifically mentioned in the Gospels, Sepphoris was a city set on a hill that was impossible to miss (Matthew 5:14). Working on the city shaped Jesus. He would have seen the Priesthood off-duty and enjoying the opulence of pagan culture. And here He would have learnt the borrowed word from Greek culture to describe the priest's behaviour: "hypocrite" or "play actor". It is possible that Jesus even worked on the construction of the huge theatre in Sepphoris. You can still see its ruins today.

Compared with what Jesus would do, being a builder on a Roman construction site was a little thing. It wasn't to be Jesus' final calling. Jesus was faithful in the little and with what belonged to another, Joseph, His father. Jesus would also have learned how to be faithful with fickle wealth.

When Joseph had left Galilee after Jesus' birth, they had been a poor family who could only afford the minimum offering for a new-born son, two doves (Leviticus 12:8, Luke 2:24). But now a builder from Nazareth would never want for paid work. Sepphoris provided a good living for skilled construction workers in wood and stone. Jesus had a skill that gave Him real value.

Now when Jesus said, "If you have not been faithful with fickle wealth, then who will trust you with the real thing?" (Luke 16:11) He used an interesting word. I translated it the same way that most Bible's do as "wealth" (or "riches"). Some Bibles don't translate the word at all they just leave it as a name, "Mammon".

"Mammon" is sometimes described as a demonic spirit of money, but this idea came about well after its use in the Bible. Jesus wouldn't have told us to be faithful with mammon if it was demonic. The word "mammon" comes from a Mishnaic Hebrew root that seems to mean something that gives you confidence, "that in which one trusts".[37]

By personifying it Jesus makes it a very personal part of the human psyche. Mammon could be *whatever* in us makes us *feel* worth it or the skills that give us the ability to draw value to us.

Jesus is not just talking about how well you use your money. There are all sorts of things people draw value from and that give them the confidence to make or attract money. Mammon could be beauty or charm; a skill or a talent; a position or title; fame or popularity.

In Jesus' case, His family's skills in the middle of a building boom made Him valuable. In a paradoxical way it was a sign of Jesus' faithfulness with mammon that He was ready to lay down His function as builder when the time came to become teacher.

More generally, if we only ever use our natural gifts and talents to strive after our own value, we will never be able to use them freely to give value.

Jesus wasn't a builder for the kudos. It was who He was in heaven; it was who He was by family inheritance; it made sense of His historic context; and it was what Jesus would do in the eternity ahead of Him, building His Church (Matthew 16:18, Ephesians 4:12) and calling us to build with Him (1 Corinthians 3:9-10).

Being a builder was not just Jesus' day job. The anointed first-born of the Father was a builder from eternity and would be one in eternity too!

Even the three and bit years when Jesus' teaching and public ministry was more in view, it was framed by the accusation that He was going to pull down and re-build the temple: at the start (John 1:19) and at the end (Matthew 27:40, Mark 15:29).

Seeing the builder deep in Jesus' essence highlights the events of Jesus' childhood and early adult life as a gift from the Father from whom every good gift comes to us all.

Striving for Christendom

At fifteen I knew I needed to find some purpose in life and in my parent's church there were young adults smuggling Bibles and living the kind of adventures I had been born into. So I started to falteringly re-engage with my Christian faith, because I knew my life needed a mission. Then I got diagnosed with cancer.

By sixteen, Jesus had healed my body of an incurable cancer, but my heart life was still very much a work in progress. Value and identity were still something I had to achieve and my healing gave me a story to dine out on in church circles.

I was asked to give my testimony at large events and both secular and Christian magazines printed my story. There was meaning and purpose in God, so I would suck up value from Him by my fervour and commitment. My zeal would define me to my peers. I would be a five talent Christian compared with all the one talent *also rans* around me. Jesus would be pleased with my five talent profit and give me more talents as a reward. I don't think I'm the only person in ministry to have ever thought like that.

As believers we have an alternative to having to create our own meaning. But our environment has shaped us and so we often find that we look to find meaning within Christendom in the same way the rest of the world does in every other sphere.

In my misshapen enthusiasm for Jesus, I wanted to quit school and become an evangelist. But my parents advised me not to rush things, to finish my schooling and go on to university. I reluctantly agreed, but with an inner proviso. I decided not to become too emotionally connected with this plan. It was my parent's idea, not mine, and I secretly hoped that God's thoughts were more like my dreams than their wisdom.

I would honour my father and mother and go to university if I had to, but it didn't really matter to me what I studied while I was there. I wasn't intending to use my degree when I had finished.

So I decided to take Philosophy, which for some reason I figured would make me a good evangelist, better able to win arguments and debates with unbelieving advocates. I enrolled in a Philosophy primer course at school and started self-studying from A.J Ayer to Zeno! But almost instantly I lost my inner peace.

The Bible expects us to have plans of our own, but they need to be kept open and flexible before Father.

"Commit your activity to the Lord and your plans will be made sure."[38] (Proverbs 16:3)

The disquiet I felt about taking Philosophy made me re-think my degree choice and this time I prayed about it. I picked Computer Science and instantly felt more comfortable with my decision. I had never studied Computers before, few had at school in the early 1980s, but I managed to swap from Philosophy to Computer Studies and started my University applications. I received two course offers, both conditional on me getting precise grades in certain subjects.

That summer during one of my physics exams, I misread a question. Pride led me to attempt an equation I wasn't being asked to solve. I failed to complete the question and ran out of time for the rest of the paper.

I've often looked back on that hour in the exam room, both kicking myself for my stupidity and stunned by how obviously providential it turned out to be for me.

I dropped two grades in Physics. I still had the right grades, but now in the wrong subjects for the courses and colleges I had applied for. I received my first college rejection, but I heard nothing in the weeks that followed from my back-up choice. Unbeknown to me, there was a rejection letter from them too, but it was in a growing pile dominated by junk mail in my father's study and he was out of the country on an extended ministry trip. By the time it came to light, universities were only a days away from re-starting and it was too late to find an alternative course.

At first I felt sick, but then I saw an exciting prospect. Perhaps Jesus didn't want me to go to university after all? Perhaps I had been right and my parents had been wrong! I had tried my best and failed to get a place, but I could still join a missions agency just as I had always wanted. My parents would have to accept this was God's plan.

But I hadn't reckoned on my mother's stubborn patience. She suggested we try one last door. I agreed to this last ditch attempt, absolutely sure I was off to join Youth With A Mission on some far-flung foreign field.

My mum rang a man in our church who worked in educational administration and the next day he came back to say that there were places available on the Computer Science degree at Royal Holloway College. I had a few days left to apply and the course started the following week.

At the time I had never even heard of Royal Holloway College and, if I had heard of it, I would not have applied there. It was small (just 1500 students) and by the Thames near Windsor, which was too close to London for my liking. And to cap it all it was under financial threat of closure, which is why it was undersubscribed that year.

Today, it's in the UK's premier division of universities. It has 12,000 plus students and worldwide recognition, not least because it featured in the novel and the film of "The Da Vinci Code".

It's hard to convey here quite how providential both the college and the Computer Science degree have been to who I am.

Obviously, I met my wife at college. And Judith has changed me for the better in ways I needed changing.

I also experienced a mini-revival at college. In my first year the Christian Union meetings had ranged from fifteen to thirty people each week. By the time I left three years later we were seeing a hundred and twenty people or more in meetings. There were salvations, deliverances, healings and people getting filled with the Holy Spirit. I remember helping to take a formal meeting in the college chapel on one occasion and seeing the organist in the balcony craning his neck backwards to see why people were shaking and falling onto the floor of the ornate Victorian sanctuary.

Things were so exciting that some of us began talking about starting a student church on campus. But life took us all in different directions.

I left Royal Holloway in 1987, changed by the experience, never intending to go back nor use the degree I had earned there. But nine years later Father bought me and Judith back into the area (Cookham is just eight miles up the River Thames from Windsor) to do a job in IT that required my degree. Seven years after that, now as leader of River Church, I oversaw the planting of the church I had dreamed about back in 1986, reaching students and staff at Royal Holloway College.

The Computer Science degree I was so ambivalent about has proved to be such a gift. Following Jesus has taken me through very distinct changes and challenges and despite not actively pursuing a career in Information Technology, at almost every major transition in my life, my "trade" has provided income and opportunities that have allowed me to take what would otherwise have been impossible steps.[39]

Looking back further I can see Father's provision in my love of playing cards and the patterns and algorithms implicit in the games and tricks I learned. I can see the assignments of the enemy shaping attitudes and expectations particularly towards education that could so easily have robbed me of opportunity.

My role as a producer-maker-builder is more multi-layered than simply maths and software. I could tell stories about my love of drama and short term jobs in theatre, but there's not the space and my stories are only here as an illustration.

You need to know who you are as a producer-maker-builder, not by your own efforts alone, but by the gifts, providence and leading of Jesus. If you know who you are in this respect already, then think about the testimony that got you to this point. Its telling has power over the devil.

So take time now to add to your story with Jesus. Do you know what you really love, the desires that make you "you"? Can you see provision in your past, in the people and events that have shaped you?

Are you happy doing what you are doing at the moment? If not, does your attitude need to change or are you doing the wrong thing for the wrong reasons?

Is there a decision you need to put before the Lord for redirection; or a past decision you need to repent from, so that He can bring you back into line with where you should be?

Before continuing ask Jesus who He has made you in the natural, then take the time to listen and write down somewhere what you believe He has said to you.

Endnotes

34. For example: "Men... begin to distinguish themselves from animals as soon as they begin to produce ... What they are, therefore, coincides with their production, both with what they produce and with how they produce..." from "The German Ideology" by Karl Marx, 1845/6.

35. This is the primary definition of "providence" given online by Dictionary. com, 2011.

36. "The "Alister Hardy Research Centre" was an academic body based, at the time, at Oxford University.

37. Encyclopedia of Religion and Ethics - 1908-1921, Volume 8:374. Editor James Hastings.

38. The verb here, "kuwn", which means to "fix", "set", "establish" etc, is in its imperfect and passive form. The imperfect form implies a process rather than an event and the passive implies that something is being done for or to you rather than by you. So this verse is saying that our openness to God allows Him to reshape and make sure our plans. It is not saying that as long as we pray about our current plans they will all happen!

39. As I write this I am actually in one of those transitions, as I leave the security of a church leader's income for a future that is still unfolding and without a regular salary. And again, despite not having done anything in IT for over eight years, just yesterday I spent the day using my skills commercially.

CHAPTER 5

THE GLORY OF CHRIST IN YOU

"At the fullness of time, God sent out His Son." (Galatians 4:4)

At some point in the summer or autumn of AD 29,[40] Jesus arrived at the Jordan to be baptised by His cousin, John. Jesus was ready and the circumstances were right.

Jesus had lived life as a favoured builder under a middle-eastern sun. But on His baptism day, the Word and the Spirit combined and Jesus emerged from the water as a teacher under an open heaven.

As prophesied by Jesus' family tree:

"The glory of God descends to dedicate a teacher."

Life under heaven has times and seasons to it. God-authored life-steps that reflect His plans for us. Some of those steps are released by anointing and revelation.

A Change of Season

Dave was a builder. Like Jesus he'd started in the trade at about the age of thirteen, but in every other respect Dave's family and social context were not like those of Jesus at all. A drop-out from "St George's School for Young Burglars", there were no prophecies or angels singing when Dave was born and no church either. Dave was an atheist a long time before he could spell it.

Dave did well as a builder and by his twenties had formed his own company with Arthur, an old school friend. Arthur had become a Christian behind Dave's back and Dave couldn't work out the change in his friend.

Dave was married by now and, while he was in Germany working on a job, his wife Gill started secretly going to church on the housing estate where they lived. Dave found out while back home one weekend and insisted on going to check out the church. First his business partner, now his wife. This wasn't funny. Dave didn't know what to expect and he certainly didn't expect what happened in the meeting. God spoke to him, three simple but unmissable words: "I know you!"

A quarter century of atheism fell at the first hurdle.

Dave soon realised he wanted to rewrite his life story and that meant going back to school. So he went to enrol at an adult education college to take GCSEs, but the tutors there persuaded him to start with A levels. Being a hotbed of political activism they suggested Politics and Sociology and two years later Dave had his first qualifications.

Dave had real favour with his teachers who encouraged him to go on and take a degree in politics at Edgefield College, linked to Lancaster University. At the end of his degree, Father spoke to Dave again, this time from the Bible: "well favoured ... with the ability to stand in the palaces of Kings; he would teach them the language and literature of the Chaldeans" (Daniel 1:4b). Dave heard a single word from heaven: "politics".

The next verse, Daniel 1:5, refers to Daniel being "educated" for three years first and Dave had just finished three years earning his degree. So he interpreted this word as God calling him straight into some kind of political mission. Dave spent £12 on political journals to look for jobs, but before he'd had a chance to open them, he knew Jesus was saying to bin them; this was God's work.

Then one of Dave's lecturers contacted him with news about a fully funded PhD at the University. Dave wasn't sure and went to the interview with an ambivalent attitude. Two hundred graduates from across Europe applied for the post. Dave, who was non-committal, was offered it. The college were shocked to say the least when Dave said he needed time to decide. God confirmed that this would be his "three years" of learning the language and literature of the political classes, so he accepted the offer.

Dave completed the research ahead of schedule and within budget.

In less than seven years Dave, the unqualified builder, had become David the university lecturer. That is the power of Word and Spirit combined; prophecy and anointing producing calling.

In David's case the glory really did dedicate him as a teacher.

But the story doesn't end there. David was due to go on a family holiday. He was about to leave his university office so checked his emails one final time before switching off the computer for a few weeks. There was an email from the British and Foreign Bible Society advertising the role of Parliamentary Officer at the Palace of Westminster. David thought it looked interesting so he hastily cobbled together a reply – then left the country.

When he returned from holiday everything changed, fast. He was offered the job. Three years learning to talk and think like a politician and now David was standing in Westminster Palace, home of the British parliament, working with MPs, civil servants, academics and the media; presenting to Lords, diplomats and even US senators; Daniel in the lion's den.

During his 10 years in Westminster, David helped establish regular prayer, worship and Bible study, and the people of God in

Parliament became bolder and more numerous.

Today, Dr David Landrum works for the Evangelical Alliance as the Director of Advocacy. Overseeing public policy, theology, research and media, he represents the concerns of Christians to Government. An anointed teacher, he's dedicated to helping Christians become civic leaders, locally and nationally.

Our best life is not released by achieving plans that we have concocted ourselves. If our lives are made for eternity, then we need to be submitted, at least in part, to heaven's perspective. After all:

"A person's way is not found in themselves: it is not in the person who walks to direct their own steps." (Jeremiah 10:23)

There is a natural season to our calling in Christ, one where we are discovering who we are in Him, as producer-maker-builders. But there is an anointed, supranatural one too, when we discover who Christ is in us.

Anointed calling is different from natural calling. Natural calling provides an apprenticeship, it is submitted to heaven's agenda. Anointed calling makes you a part of heaven's agenda, exercising a different kind of authority from a submitted heart. Anointed calling often brings together the disparate inputs of heaven into your past life and shapes them into a new whole; Spirit-soaked, not just inspired.

The Glory on You

As Jesus came up out of the Jordan, heaven opened and the Holy Spirit who had been *in* Him and *with* Him His whole earthly life came on Jesus in a fresh way.

The Spirit is like the wind, hard to tie down. Creating dogmas on how the Spirit should work can be divisive and limiting. I don't want to be too precise, but I have found it helpful to see the differences in role and action of the Spirit *in, on* and *with* us.[41]

If we are involved with deliberate missions work we'll often encounter the Spirit *with* us. The Holy Spirit has been out evangelising way before we arrive, but our cooperation acts as a touch point, turning the Spirit's breeze into a concrete encounter. Now, even after the Spirit has come *on* us, we don't stop cooperating with the Spirit *with* us, which is why we read, even after Jesus' baptism that:

"The power of the Lord was *with* Him to heal them." (Luke 5:17b)

But anointed calling has far more to do with the interaction of the Spirit that comes *on* us with the Spirit that is already *in* us. In the Old Testament, when the Spirit came on people they did something remarkable and then the Spirit lifted from them. But in the New Testament when the Spirit comes on you it activates something in the Spirit that's *in* you, a gift or a ministry. The Spirit in us draws energy from the Spirit on us. Prophecies and promises get re-made and turned on.

When the bits in us that have been put there or activated over the years by the Spirit on us all come together, we see an anointed life.

The Spirit had been in Jesus from conception, but when the Spirit came on Him it released a new season under heaven.

"This is My Son, beloved (David), in whom I am very pleased." (Matthew 3:17)

These words are marvellously multi-layered. We saw in *The Supra-Natural Life* how they were a word of truth, of love and of favour. But they also spoke into Jesus' value, identity and His calling.

The phrase "My Son" is from Psalm 2:7 and was a recognised title of the Messiah, as was "Son of David", and "David" means "beloved" in Hebrew and Aramaic. And as a "beloved Son" the Father valued Jesus.

But there was third part to the sentence, one that spoke to Jesus' calling. He might be the Messiah, but what did that mean in terms of how Jesus should be and act? "In whom I'm very pleased" gave Jesus a clue.

The phrase is from the Septuagint, the Greek language version of the Old Testament used in Jesus' day. It described the "suffering servant", foreseen by the prophet Isaiah (Isaiah 44:1).[42]

Nobody had ever put the ideas attached to the suffering servant together with the identity of the Messiah before. Kings reign, fight wars and are served, but the suffering servant was compassionate, obedient, caring for others' needs. He would use sharp words to bring Israel back to God and He would become a "covenant" to them. Most famously, this servant would suffer and die on behalf of others whose wellbeing He was securing.

Father's word over Jesus gave him both the "who" and the "how" of His identity and calling.

Of course, it wasn't as if all of this was brand new to Jesus. He knew who His family were and their connection to King David. Mary had been specifically told by the Angel Gabriel that her Son was the "Son of the Most High" and a descendant of David (Luke 1:32) and she must have told Jesus these things.

When Jesus was just a month old He had been taken to the Temple where an old man, Simeon, had prophesied over Him that He would be a "Light to the Gentiles." The exact phrase comes from Isaiah 42:6, the same passage quoted over Jesus by His heavenly Father at His baptism.

Isaiah uses the concept of light coming to the Gentile nations a few times, the first being in reference to the virgin-born child's adult destiny (Isaiah 9:1-2). Mary, who pondered these things (Luke 2:19), would have sown these seeds into the growing Jesus.

In the first chapter of this book we saw how Simon became Peter. Revelation activated a truth he had already heard from his flesh and blood family. It seems that Peter's experience mirrored something of Jesus' experience, whose family had also told Him who He was. Second hand revelation is just information until it gets picked up by a fresh, direct word. But the direct word from heaven can draw on all the meaning already laid down in us by friends, family, and history.

At His baptism Jesus was being commissioned as an Heir, not just affirmed as a Son. He was moving from promise to practice.

The Usual Pattern of Events

It all sounds very neat when spelt out in less than half a chapter: the Spirit comes on you, unlocks something in you, bang! New life-stage. Life is seldom simple, but messy truth is often best communicated by neat patterns that we can use as rough guides. Because messy patterns are too hard to follow.

So the breakthrough from natural to anointed calling often unfolds over time, in overlapping or parallel stages or seemingly out of order. The Spirit might come on you several times to release the same gift or stage. To complicate things further, there are sub-stages of calling too. In Jesus' ministry as an anointed teacher we see the Holy Spirit releasing a sub-stage in Him at His Transfiguration[43] and the night before His Crucifixion.[44]

At one level it's true that the Spirit simply came on Jesus and a new phase of life started. But the Spirit acted in a moment on things sown into Jesus over thirty years. And then there was a nine-month period between Jesus' baptism and the start of His full-time public ministry in Galilee.

Father's plan for us is His initiative, but it can be resisted, rejected or left as an unopened gift. Jesus shows us how to receive it, fight for it and cooperate with it.

Straight after His baptism, the Spirit led Jesus into the desert; a God-initiated time of wrestling with the promise and with the devil that settled the implications of the word and anointing in Jesus.

"If you are the Son of God, turn these rocks into bread" (Matthew 4:3) is a challenge to test whether there is authority in Jesus' identity. But a servant serves others before he serves his own needs. One day Jesus would turn water into wine and multiply bread and fish, but as a value-adder not as a value-grabber; as a producer not as a consumer.

"God won't let you fall no matter how outrageous you are…" (based on Luke 4:11) is a temptation to make a showy display of Jesus' value to the Father, whereas the suffering servant is described as not self-publicising (Isaiah 42:2 etc).

The nations are given to "My Son" by the Father (Psalm 2:8). Jesus shouldn't need to ask the devil for them. Even more importantly, the suffering servant attracted the nation by His light through acts of service and healing (Isaiah 42:7). The temptation was to win the world without the cross but, as we shall see, there is always an element of suffering in anointed calling. Not because God is a sadist, but because being anointed is sustained by intimacy and you can't get close to the heart of God without feeling as He feels; great joy, but great pain too.

Jesus doesn't rush into a new phase of life. He is deliberate in letting it grow under heaven's glory. At first He stays by the Jordan, learning from John the Baptist and experimenting with the miraculous. Jesus becomes a teacher to a few disciples in private. The first time Jesus speaks to a crowd they've come for the feast in Jerusalem, not to hear Him (John 2).

But through this period Jesus would have been very aware of a truth trapped between the prophecies of His birth and baptism. The "Light to the Gentiles" was called to minister at the edge, in Galilee (Isaiah 9:1-2).

Around nine months after His baptism, Jesus set out for home, travelling through Samaria. At about this time, John the Baptist was arrested. The arrest was a sign to Jesus that the time for His role as anointed teacher had arrived in earnest, so:

"Jesus returned in the power of the Spirit into Galilee, and news about Him spread through all the surrounding area. And He began teaching in their synagogues and was praised by all." (Luke 4:14-15)

Jesus is now a teacher and the world would almost forget He was ever a builder.

The anointing happened in a moment, but its effect took time to gestate. It is important to see this, because this is how anointed callings tend to grow in us – even when we get everything right. Add our mistakes and stubbornness into the mix and we create the complex harmonies of real life out of the simple tunes heaven hums over us.

The seasons of faithfulness – with our natural gifts, the little things, and with other peoples' calling – are so important. They teach us how to consolidate the Word and Spirit in us, so when we are revealed as heirs (Romans 8:19) we know how to behave with the identity and value we've been given.

Anointed Calling

In *The Supra-Natural Life* I described an experience I had while praying on the toilet back in the first few years of the new millennium. Thankfully the room didn't shake, but God had definitely spoken a word and the Spirit was on it, or on me, or perhaps both. That word ultimately led me out of IT and into ministry, with a fresh ability to hear Jesus and a new authority in healing.

The event was key, but it was neither the first capital letter nor the final full stop in the story that has bought me into a more obviously anointed style of life.

Another key point came in 2008 when the Holy Spirit came on me in a worship time to the degree that I was bouncing off the floor. With hindsight I can see that that "anointing" precipitated a chain of events, some good, some bad, some happy, some sad, that would lead me out of the role I had in church and into the more eclectic role I have now. And, on the journey, I saw the clearest fulfilments to date of the first word I can remember ever receiving from God. It came via a bit of a struggle, by reading the Bible and with some help from a friend.

Jeremiah 1:4-8 is marked in my Bible and dated, "31st August 1981" with the phrase "I was asking God what I ought to do." It was the first thing I ever wrote in my wide margin study Bible and it was actually transferred from a previous Sunday School Bible. The date is seven months before I was diagnosed with cancer, the point I had decided I would follow Jesus. I wanted Him to talk to me, but I couldn't get anything. So I would open the Bible at random and because Jeremiah is a big book and in about the middle, Jeremiah is what I got. I didn't understand the random verses I was reading and a friend suggested I should try reading from the beginning of the book. Verse 7 caught my attention: "Don't say I am only youth." I claimed the verses for myself. I can't say I was sure God had spoken, I just wanted Him to have spoken, so I highlighted them in the Bible I was using. In particular I highlighted verse 5, "I will make you a prophet to nations."

Now since my Holy Spirit shaking experience in 2008 there have been various events in my life that have expressed the idea of being a prophet in my own nation. I've hosted a 24-hour national leaders' retreat in Windsor Castle, the Queen's main residence. I can't say much more as I had to sign a confidentiality contract to use the venue. In 2010 I gave a written prophetic word to a small group of leaders. The word cascaded and multiplied by word of mouth and became the foundation of a 1,000-leader event in Westminster in 2011, which many see as marking the start of a new season in the UK Church. I've also shared my healing testimony with the Danish Ambassadors to the UK and I've helped convene a time for national "elders" in the Houses of Parliament to listen to the Lord on behalf of the nation.

I've been deliberately brief in my descriptions. I don't want them to sound like successes to emulate; they didn't feel that way when they happened. But if nothing else happens, I would feel sure that in these events Jesus had honoured this first word I ever claimed for myself.

In a quiet way there has been glory in the process, but it would be unbalanced not to mention the cost too.

I'm discovering a joy in anointed calling, but paradoxically I'm finding that there is a lot of discomfort and pain in the journey as well. Paul writes about the tension of glory and suffering all the time, and it was for the joy set before Him that Jesus endured the cross.

I'm not talking about a self-inflicted or masochistically enjoyed suffering. There have, of course, been all sorts of odd and unhelpful theologies of suffering. But it is a shallow theology that does not address this genuine part of God's experience.

I've found real insights into the paradox in Paul's letters. Paul sees suffering as a privileged part of the called out and anointed life. Because the anointed life is more about who Christ is in you, than it is about who you are in Christ. And, of course, Christ suffered for the sins of the world. So:

"The sufferings of this present time are not worthy to be compared with the glory which will be revealed in us." (Romans 8:18b)

The Glory of "Christ in You."

Paul gives us insight into his own calling in his letter to the Colossian church:

"I was made a minister (in line with the stewardship from God committed to me for your benefit), *to fulfil the word of God.*" (Colossians 1:25)[45]

Paul was called Saul when he met Jesus on the road to Damascus. Jesus didn't change Saul's name for him,[46] as he did with Simon, but the call He spoke into Saul so radically changed this young man's career plans that in time, the Roman name "Paul", which means "Small" would seem more appropriate than "Saul", the Jewish King who had pursued God's anointed with a murderous heart.

What Jesus did say was that Saul would be a "minister and a witness";[47] a witness to things that Jesus would reveal to Paul over the course of his life to come (Acts 26:16).

Now the letter to the Colossian church is evenly split into

practical pastoral advice and deep truth about the divine Christ. So by writing this letter Paul was fulfilling Jesus' word into him from that first meeting. He was ministering practically into the church and bearing witness to the things Jesus has shown him of His divine nature.

Paul's life was a fulfilment of the word of Jesus to Saul, just as Peter's life was a fulfilment of Jesus' word to Simon. But there is something more, because Jesus doesn't just speak the word of God, He is the "Word of God" (John 1:1); and He lives in us!

Jesus is the author, the promise and the fulfilment of the word to us. So Paul continues:

"This mystery, hidden from ages and generations but now revealed in His saints:[48] to whom God wanted to make known what is the rich value of the glory of this mystery! Which is: *'Christ in You', the hope of glory."* (Colossians 1:26-27)

At the start of this book Paul was praying for enlightenment for us to discover the "rich value of the glory of Jesus' inheritance" in us. Here Paul reveals that the rich valuable inheritance is wrapped up in the "mystery" of "Christ in you." A mystery so intrinsic to Paul's preaching and our calling that in the next verse he refers to it as:

"The thing we proclaim, drawing everyone's attention to it; and teaching everyone in all wisdom, so that we may present everyone complete in Christ Jesus." (Colossians 1:25-28)

Paul uses the word "mystery" twenty times in his letters to describe the Gospel message he preached. The modern Church has managed to package the Gospel into four-point lists of things to be believed and be saved by – but we shouldn't mistake the simplicity of the message for the profound mystery of its reality.

Many followers of Jesus consign the ideas of "Christ in them" to the realm of spiritual language and words; liturgies and sound bites to recite and polish while they get on with the serious business of holiness. But Paul tells us he is not interested in fancy words that can't be demonstrated by the Spirit with power (1 Corinthians 2:4). **Christ in you is a real experience, not just a nice idea.**

The pains, victories and patterns of Christ's life replay and rewrite themselves in His people time and time again. Jesus said that the Word of God could produce fruit a hundred fold; in other words it multiplies. So it shouldn't surprise us that as the Word of God, Christ's life multiplies itself in us.

For instance, last year a loved friend of mine died.

I stood outside the emergency room with his wife, their four-month-old baby girl and his gathering family, "a man of sorrows acquainted with grief." We joined hands and commanded his heart to restart in the name of Jesus. And it did; all on its own; "Lazarus come forth."

In total, Phil was dead for twelve and a half minutes that night. Even with his miraculous heart restart the medics expected permanent brain damage. But there is none and just before Christmas, when he was signed off by the hospital, they told him that his heart was now stronger and more regular than when he had first visited the doctor with a broken foot – the incident that led to the thrombosis that led to the massive heart attack that killed him.

I will tell the full story in the next book in this series as it contains lessons on faith and favour, the subject of the book three. But I'm telling it here because it is such a clear and concrete example to me of how real aspects of our lives connect with Christ and His life. Even as I write this, I can feel the connection with Jesus standing outside a communal grave with friends and family. Jesus is the hope of glory every time we pray for a miracle.

You may have started to notice this connection in your own life-defining stories and moments too. The inner life of Jesus that empowered the stories we read in the Gospels is in you, by faith, even when you don't feel it, ready to rise up and recapitulate its victories of grace and truth. It is a mystery, but with very powerful and real implications.

The problem is that we have become so familiar with the doctrinal idea of "Christ in you" that it no longer seems like a mystery. We have sung songs about Jesus living in us since childhood or salvation and we have become inoculated to the power that comes from actively unravelling and solving the mystery in us.

Paul uses the word "mystery" not because the ideas are hard to understand, but because the meaning of the Gospel in you is unknowable until you actually live the adventure you were saved for.

This is why Paul comments that it is only "now" being revealed in the diversity of different cultures and people receiving Christ and stepping into their inheritance. Christ's inheritance in the saints will one day encompass the world and every fruitful and constructive human endeavour.

Claiming your Inheritance

"The Lord spoke to Joshua the son of Nun ... every place on which the sole of your foot treads, I have given it to you." (Joshua 1:1b-3)

Joshua is a form of the name "Yeshua", "Jesus" in its original Hebrew form, and Joshua's father's name, "Nun", means "eternal".[49] Prophetically, the book of Joshua is addressed to "Jesus the eternal son." The whole book is about Jesus' inheritance in the Saints and how He will fill all things (Ephesians 4:10) through His corporate body, you and me.

By Christ in us we become:

"A stewardship appropriate to the fullness of the season, summing up all things in Christ, things in the heavens and things on the earth. Also in Him we have obtained/become an inheritance." (Ephesians 1:10-11a)

Translators are undecided as to how Verse 11 above should be translated: "we have obtained an inheritance" or "we have become an inheritance." The ambiguity is not surprising and may be deliberate on Paul's part. Later in his letter Paul deliberately misquotes a Psalm when he says, "He gave gifts to Men" (Ephesians 4:8); instead of "He received gifts from Men" (Psalm 68:18). I guess ambiguity is part of the quality of a mystery, whether it's quantum mechanics or the union of Christ in His Church. Deep reality doesn't fit easily into everyday language.

Now as Joshua the son of Nun occupied the Promised Land, each Israelite family had its own portion, a plot with their name on it. And, as Jesus the Eternal Son fills up all things, He will do so through the feet and hands of those willing to accept their calling from Him. As Paul observed, while we are all heirs of God, it is the mature that are co-heirs with Christ (Romans 8:17).[50] Accepting your calling from Him is part of that maturity. That's why it's the meek who "inherit the Earth" (Matthew 5:5). Doing incredible things out of obedience is not the same as doing them to prove something.

But we shouldn't think that accepting Jesus' call and being conformed to His image is restrictive; it is a doorway into a house of many rooms. There is an incredible diversity in His unity.

Trinity Dancing

"Christ in You" is a truth attained by the release of glory in us by the glory on us.

"And the Glory which You have given Me, I have given to them; So that they may be one in the way that We are one. I in them and You in Me." (John 17:22-23)

And glory speaks about the Holy Spirit, because "glory" seems to be a particular quality or attribute the Spirit brings to the mix.

"The Spirit of Glory and of God rests on you." (1 Peter 4:14b)

Of course, the Father and Son have glory too, perhaps because the Spirit, the energising life and essence of the Godhead, pervades and encompasses them both in their tri-unity. In the Godhead the Holy Spirit is the love between the lover and the beloved; the gift between the giver and the receiver.

"Christ in You" is a mystery because it connects us to the deepest reality in the Godhead, the Trinity. The one-ness of Christ and His people is like the glorious one-ness of Father, Son and Holy Spirit.

"The Lord your God is One."[51] (Deuteronomy 6:4)

The Hebrew word for "one" used in this verse is not the word for a single object, it is the word for a unit. It is the same word used when it says of marriage that "the two will become *one* flesh" (Genesis 2:24).

God is a unity of entangled and distinct parts.

The Trinity is one of the most beautiful ideas that can be thought. The oneness-in-diversity which is God's nature is extended into humanity by our union with Christ; His Church is His Body is His Bride.

Jesus brings us into the divine dynamic dance that is God, a truth the early Church fathers called the "perichoresis"[52] or the "dancing around-ness of God."

Peter explains how the process of being brought into that dance works. It is:

"...by the means of fully knowing Him who called us to glory and excellence, by this means we are given the biggest and most precious promises: That by these you become participators of the divine nature..." (2 Peter 1:3-4a)

The hope of our calling binds the earthiness of our natural identity into the divine nature. Creation is summed up in Christ as our earthly feet come into contact with every inch of it. We join frustrated creation to the fruitful plans of heaven.

For Peter, these words were more than theory or homily. They describe exactly how he, and Paul, had come into their biggest and most precious promises. They had both seen Jesus by revelation, not just naturally; and in this they had heard and understood his personal calling to glory and excellence. As they cooperated with this promise they found themselves entangled with Jesus' divine nature in their own unique ways.

In *The Supra-Natural Life* we unpacked Paul's teaching in Romans chapter eight. We explored how the Holy Spirit effectively intervened (v26) on our behalf and looked for our cooperation (v28) to "conform" us, in line with the purpose of the calling on us, to the "image of His Son" (v29).

Paradoxically, being conformed to the image of Christ releases our uniqueness; it does not make us all the same!

This same paradox is in the Trinity too: Father, Son and Holy Spirit entangled as One, but each member is different in function, personality and expression. None can be unravelled from the others or fully understood on their own.[53] So Jesus was the image of the invisible God (Father, Son and Holy Spirit) and at the same time He is unique and distinct as the Son.

Before Simon was "the Rock", Jesus had already been the rock. According to Paul (who presumably was shown it by Jesus), Jesus was the rock that followed Moses in the wilderness (1 Corinthians 10:4); He was David's rock of refuge (Psalm 61:2); and as Peter himself acknowledges, He was the true foundation stone of the Church, rejected by men and a stumbling block to some (1 Peter 2:6-8).

Simon could be "Peter" because Christ in Him was also a rock. But Simon was also uniquely Simon.

The Lord is more interested in you becoming who you were made to become, than you doing what needs to be done! There are aspects of the life Father has dreamed for you that will not be found in you yourself, because they've been hidden with Christ in God (Colossians 3:3).

We pursue our natural calling by faith, but as we pursue the presence of Jesus, His faithfulness delivers on the promises we have received, promises that go beyond the natural.

"We all, with unveiled face beholding as in a mirror the glory of the Lord, are transformed into the same image from glory to glory…" (2 Corinthians 3:18)

So as we look to uncover the unique value, identity and calling of Christ in us and us in Christ, we will continually find elements of Christ's story in us and see our story in His. We may even discover bits of others who are "in Christ" whose stories seem to be "in us" too! That happens a lot as you read the Bible.

Can you see any connection points between you and the life of Jesus? Ask Him to show you the connection points. Then ask Him to help you feel like He feels. If you have time, start to re-read the Gospels asking yourself the question, "What was Jesus thinking?" If you can't answer that question, ask yourself, "What would I have been thinking if I were Jesus?" These are the ways we see Him more clearly; the way He changes us from glory to glory.

Also, try to remember any past words from God that almost seem irrelevant; they have a habit of coming back when you least expect them.

Finally, I would encourage you to go to places where the Spirit is moving. It's what Jesus did, spending time at John the Baptist's campaign. It was what I was doing the day I got shaken and stirred. It's not vital, as Paul's experience shows, but Father honours our hunger for Him. It's those that seek who find and those that knock who have the door opened to them (Luke 11:10).

In you, glory can release Christ the banker, nurse, mechanic, doctor, software engineer .... you can fill in the blank.

Endnotes

40. Luke tells us that John the Baptist started baptising in the 15th year of Tiberias. While there are various ways of understanding when the first year of an emperor's reign might start, we must remember that Luke was writing to a Roman audience, so would use the standard Roman system. AD29 seems to be confirmed by John's Gospel where at Jesus' first Passover He is told that the sanctum of the temple has been standing for 46 years, during which time the outer temple had been in continuous construction. The sanctum was completed in 18 or 17 BC, so this statement makes sense if made in 30AD.

41. See the chapter, "Truly, Newly Human" in *The Supra-Natural Life*.

42. Modern English versions don't use the Septuagint as a primary source for

the Old Testament, so in Isaiah they tend to translate the phrase as something like: "in whom my soul delights".

43. At His Transfiguration, the Galilean Prophet becomes the Jewish Messiah. Jesus glows with glory as He is enveloped by cloud. The Father speaks over Jesus again.

44. On the night Jesus died He specifically prays about receiving back the glory He had in the beginning (John 17:5). Then, when He declares, "I am", the soldiers fall backwards, struck by the glory of God. At the Crucifixion the Jewish Messiah becomes the World's Saviour.

45. Some translations add words to create a phrase like "I have completely preached the word of God." There is no need for this if we understand the importance placed by the early Church on the prophetic as a way of embodying Jesus, who was the Word of God made flesh.

46. It is possible that Paul was already part of Saul's full name as we know he was a Roman citizen and, as such, had three names: a local given name, probably Saul; a Roman name to be known by, probably Paul; and a formal Roman name, which we don't know, perhaps because the formal name was often taken from the famous Roman who had originally sponsored a family's adoption into citizenship and Paul would rather be known as "small" than make claims to grandeur with a moniker linked to a pagan ruler. The Bible calls Paul "Saul" up to the point he starts his missionary work, after which it is more pragmatic to use his Roman name.

47. Paul gives us three accounts of his meeting with Jesus on the road to Damascus and the revelations and words bought to him. These words came both instantly and over the next few days, by direct revelation and by another Christian, Ananias. As well as being told he would be a minister and a witness, Paul was told that this would be to both Jews and gentiles and to Kings. Jesus promised Paul theological revelation.

48. Almost every English Bible translates this phrase "to His Saints", but the Greek contains no explicit preposition. The noun phrase is simply in the dative case, so the whole phrase could be equally translated "by", "with" or "in" as well as "to". As the mystery that is being revealed is the consequence of "Christ in you" it would seem that "in His Saints" fits the flow of Paul's argument better than "to His Saints", although the latter is undoubtedly true as well.

49. The name "Nun" is most often translated as "fish", but Hitchcock' Bible Names Dictionary also gives "Posterity" or "Eternal" as options.

50. See The Supra-Natural Life for a full treatment of this verse.

51. The word for "one" used in Deuteronomy above is "echad", which can mean

"a unit" or "a unity". It is not the simple word for a unique one, "yachiyd". "Echad" is the word used when it says of man and woman, "they will become one flesh" (Genesis 2:24); it is a unit made of parts.

52. "Perichoresis" was a term for the Trinity first coined by Gregory of Nazianzas, a theologian and bishop of Constantinople in the mid 4th century AD.

53. You get an immediate sense that the members of the Trinity are unique if you try to reverse the way you speak about them. So you can say, "God the Father", "God the Son" and "God the Spirit", and you can also say "Son of God" and "Spirit of God", but you wouldn't say "Father of God"! There is a quality to the Father that is different from the Son and Spirit that doesn't allow it!

CHAPTER 6
THE SECRETLY WONDERFUL NAME

"I have redeemed you; I have called you by name, you are Mine." (Isaiah 43:1b)

When God says to Moses, "I have known you by name" (Exodus 33:17), He is stating something far deeper than simply that He knows the syllables and letters that make up the label attached to the man.

Conceptually, as we have already seen, there is a connection in Hebrew thinking between Heaven ("*sham*ayim"); the gust of glory breathed into us ("ne*shem*ah"); and our name ("*shem*"). They are all connected to the Hebrew root word "sh-m", which conveys the idea of essence; our intrinsic value and nature. So it is not surprising that so many people find their name gets changed as the Spirit of glory transforms them.

When the glory of God descended to dedicate Jesus as a teacher, the Gospels tell us that the heavens were opened up in a new way to Jesus.[54] As a result, "Yeshua ben-Yosef" became "Jesus Christ", the world's most recognised name.

Generally in the ancient world, name changes were expected when somebody stepped up into a position with a lot of power and authority. Gaius Octavius became Caesar Augustus. Note how the title becomes a part of the name.

The Bible gives us plenty of examples of how a God-given name can reflect the change in someone or be part of the process of change in someone.

Sometimes the name change is a small modification, like Sarai becoming Sarah (Genesis 17:15). Other times the change is total, like Simon becoming Peter. Sometimes God explicitly gives the name change, as when Jacob becomes Israel (Genesis 32:27-28). And other times it just seems to happen because God deals with or uses a person in a particular way, such as when Moses renames Hoshea as Joshua (Numbers 13:16). Then, of course, there are the times when God takes the initiative to give a person their name from birth.

While they are not magic, names are important. The ancient world knew it and the Romans had a phrase for it, "Nomen est omen" which means "the name is a prophetic sign."

In 1994 New Scientist magazine coined the phrase "Nominative Determinism" to describe the phenomenon of behaviours or career choices that seem to have been influenced by a person's name. But over forty years before the New Scientist article, psychologist Karl Jung had already noted the "sometimes quite grotesque coincidence between a man's name and his peculiarities."[55]

New Scientist's first article on the shaping power of names cited a paper on incontinence in the British Journal of Urology, written by the unbelievably named A. J. Splatt and D. Weedon. They revisited the subject earlier this year referring to a paper on "Plasmodium Transmission in Alaskan Bird Populations" by a C. Loiseau proving the phenomenon is no respecter of language (L'oiseau is French for "the bird"). Just for the fun of it, it's worth pointing out that Pan-Am Airlines was founded by Juan Trippe. The Managing Director of dairy company Danone in the UK is called Bruno Fromage. There is prison reformer with the name Frances Crooke (Frances means "Free", so her name means "Free Criminals"). The current Lord Chief Justice of England and Wales is a Judge Judge. In 2011, Rich Ricci of Barclays Bank was given a £44 million bonus. And there is, in all seriousness, a vasectomy doctor in Texas called Richard Chopp.

Every now and then serious psychologists write serious papers to try and explain nominative determinism. They usually fail and end up amusing themselves by circulating their latest finds to each other or sending a letter to New Scientist. But ignoring the funny and bizarre there does seem to be a real dynamic at work. There are disproportionate numbers of "Dr Doctor" and dentists called "Denis" or "Denise".[56] Natural sciences can only go partway to understanding what's happening here; to really get a feel we need to open ourselves up to the prophetic and the supra-natural.

Rock Solid

It was June 18th 2006: a pretty usual Sunday. I had spoken at our church when, at the end of the service, I was approached by my friend Carol to ask if I would go and pray for someone. "Shaky Dave" as he was known, was a relatively new believer. He had introduced himself as "Shaky Dave" when he first joined our church's Alpha course. It was what everyone around town called him as he suffered from Parkinson's disease. Dave had given his life to Jesus on that Alpha course and he had had an incredible breakthrough in his mental health. Over the years his physical condition had left him very depressed, but the depression lifted off him when Dave received Jesus.

Dave's physical symptoms were severe and had been for a long time. His shaking had caused him to lose his long-term partner and his job as the landlord of a large pub in the centre of town. Dave had to use a stick to help him walk. So it wasn't surprising that he had fallen into depression. But in the time I had known Dave he had been very positive, so it was a surprise to see him looking so low that Sunday morning.

Dave burst into tears as I approached. "I'm sick of this disease," he told me. "I saw my doctor two weeks ago and there is nothing more they can do for me. I'm on the highest medication. The doctor just said I have to get on with life."

I guess I knew what was coming next and I also knew that I didn't have the faith for it. Then Shaky Dave said it: "Please will you pray for me to be healed." I called over a friend, Jon. Jon had been healed a couple of months before after several years of debilitating ME; perhaps he would have some faith. (He told me later that he didn't!)

So I laid a hand on Shaky Dave and was hit by an immediate conviction or rebuke from the Lord. "You should never have called him 'Shaky Dave'." I felt the pain of it in my stomach.

So instead of praying for his healing, I found myself repenting out loud for calling Dave "Shaky" and, as I repented, I found myself prophesying over him. "You will no longer be called 'Shaky Dave', but you will be called 'Rock Solid Dave' because you are a faithful friend and the Lord commends you for it."

As I prophesied I felt a greater boldness to pray for Dave's healing, but nothing seemed to happen. I'll let Dave finish the story in his words:

"At the time I didn't think much of it. I'd had a lot of prayer since joining the church. There had been times I'd felt better as a result, but to no major effect. This time seemed no different. When I got up the next day I noticed something had changed. Whereas I usually staggered to the bathroom like a Thunderbird puppet, today I walked steadily – something I hadn't done for eight years! At first I thought it was just one of my good days, even if it was significantly better than any I'd had for years. I was dressed and breakfasted and took my dog, George, for a walk. It was as though George knew there was something different too as he started to run up the road whilst on the lead. I managed to run with him! I didn't dare believe it would last, so I didn't tell anyone, but really enjoyed the day."

Rock Solid Dave started to tell people what had happened to him on the Wednesday. His shaking had stopped, the effects of Parkinson's were gone. People who know Dave's story call him "Rock Solid."

It's important to finish the story. Two years ago David was diagnosed with an inoperable cancer and sent home to die. His shaking returned. A year later Dave is in remission from the cancer, though he is still shaking. I don't fully understand the complex relationship between sicknesses and our psyches, but neither do I want to lose sight of the fact that, for several years, Dave walked in a healing related to a change in his name.

Isaiah prophesied to us all when he prophesied to Jerusalem:

"The nations shall see your righteousness, and all kings your glory, and you shall be called by a *new name*, which the mouth of the Lord shall pronounce." (Isaiah 62:2)

In this verse the word "name" is a different word from the more usual "shem", but it illustrates something of the spiritual dynamics of God giving us a new name. The Hebrew word is "naqab", the root means to "pierce through", "drill through" or "cut through", but it is used figuratively to mean a word that cuts right into someone's whole being.

You see, that's what happens with a name. It gets into the deepest parts of who we are for good or for ill. Because we allow ourselves to be indentified by our name it will produce fruit in us. Which is why it is important we hear the name God knows us by.

The world will see our glory and God will speak a name over us, one that cuts to the heart of who we are; that changes us from the very core of our inner-self. It is part of our experience as an overcomer.

"To the one who overcomes, I will give hidden manna and I will give them a white stone, and on the stone is written a *new name*, which no one knows but the one who receives it." (Revelation 2:17)

The overcomer has a new name, a name written on a white stone and given in the context of hidden manna.

Manna speaks about fresh daily revelation.[57] The fact that this particular manna is hidden manna speaks about the private life of communion that exists between the overcomer and Jesus.

In the ancient world a white stone was given as a sign of freedom from guilt at the end of a trial. So a white stone speaks about our freedom from sin, freedom from where we have come from.

And in the ancient world, a stone of any colour with a name on it acted as an access ticket to the named event or as the freedom of the city or context named.

John mixes up the two ideas. You are free *from* your past and you are free *for* your future. The new identity reflected in a new name is captured in a symbol that speaks about your journey – Jesus gives us a testimony stone.

One last thing about that white stone: according to Exodus 16:31, manna looked like white coriander seed and tasted like honey. Coriander seeds are about 4mm in diameter, so manna must have looked like pearls and a big piece of manna must have looked like a white pebble.

Our new name is processed into us as part of our hidden manna, our private dialogue with the Lord, even if we received a part of that name publicly, by prophecy or from our parents. Like Simon we need to be heaven hearers to receive our new name, which should encourage us to talk to the Lord about our story, the white stone of testimony.

So I want to think about hidden manna before we explore the new name it produces.

Hidden Manna

It's amusing watching really old sci-fi films. They imagined the future as a cleaner, faster and more comfortable version of the 1960s and 70s. Back then nobody anticipated the changes to life brought about by mobile phones, the Internet, ebooks, Facebook, and the like. The connectedness of the digital world has changed us. In the coming years we will see driverless cars, bins that request waste services and who knows what else.

When the glory of God descended onto Jesus it opened a connection with heaven, and it is a characteristic of the anointed phase of life that we live out of the connection the cross has opened up for us, not just from the fresh start it has won for us. This connectedness should change life even more radically than the invention of the smart phone, but too often we approach our new life as if it's just a second stab at the old one.

It's like having a mobile phone but keeping it at home and only turning it on for a few minutes a day or when you need to call someone, which is what I did when I got my first cell phone.

But now my smart phone goes everywhere with me and is constantly ringing, buzzing and shaking as it tweets me, pokes me, texts me and guides me to the nearest restaurant.

The Spirit that Jesus has put in me responds to the Spirit on me and around me. The Lord wants to prompt us, talk with us and guide us all day everyday. The anointed life is lived in constant communion; a two-way dialogue, not just a monologue at God.

Through this connection, Jesus redeems, fixes and activates every part of us: new emotions come on; new spiritual sensitivity gets activated; purpose emerges from what looked like random personal history.

This is our daily bread.

The more we eat the bread of His presence, the more we discover God's love and purposes in the minutia of life.

So life under an open heaven is not necessarily made up of big significant events. But it is a life that knows the value and purpose in every twist and turn of the journey. As we saw, futility is not the lack of an action or a goal; it is the lack of connection to God's plans and purpose. The most grandiose and extravagant actions can be full of sound and fury but signify nothing[58] (or at least very little), whilst little things can be rich with the pleasure and purpose of heaven.

Today I received a text message from one of my daughters. It was a single letter "k". In itself the letter "k" means very little, but in the bigger context of our relationship it meant a great deal. It was short for "Ok" and "Ok" was the response to an earlier request. It was our relationship and our conversations that gave that single letter meaning and purpose and made me feel happy. At the same time the letter 'k" extended the very relationship that gave it its meaning.

And so it is between us and Father. In the context of our relationship and dialogue, a little thing can take on a big significance. A song comes onto the radio, one that I have told Jesus I really like; or I ask Him for a parking space and some one pulls out just as I drive up. Because I am in dialogue with God, these moments of synchronicity stop being background noise; our connection means they become divine co-incidents, post-it note communication to me of my value to a Father whose face is turned towards me.

It is easy to say, "Well those things would probably have happened anyway" and perhaps that is true, but as our intimacy with Father increases, we will start to recognise the truth in practice, not just theory, of the verse that says:

"Every good gift and every perfect gift is from above, coming down from the Father of lights." (James 1:17)

The more sure you are of His love for you the more thankful you will be for every small blessing; the more you see small blessings the more you are sure of His love for you. This attitude is not naïve but it is self-catalysing; the more you believe it the more you will see it and the more that you see it the more you will believe it. It seems naïve to those that don't live this way, but energises those that do.

The foundation of the life you were made for is communion with God. And it's in this context that we receive the white stone with the secretly wonderful name on it.

The Piece of God That Surpasses Understanding

Now as we read on in Revelation we discover a wonderful ambiguity, the new name we receive seems to belong to both Jesus who is speaking and to the overcomer who receives it. What's more it is no longer written on a small white stone, it is now written on the overcomer who has become a big chunk of marble in God's new house.

"He who overcomes, I will make a pillar in the temple of My God ... I will write on them the name of my God, and the name of the city of my God, the new Jerusalem ... and my own new name." (Revelation 3:12)

Our new identity is always entangled with the truth of Christ in us. Take a quick look at the people to whom God gave a new name and you will notice that their new name almost always includes a piece of God:

Jacob became Israel and Israel contains God's name "El"; Joshua adds the "Jah" sound, the shortened name of God, to his old name Hoshea; Abram and Sarai get the "ah" of "Jah" added to their names. Even Simon's new name, "Rock", is a title given to Jesus, the Rock of refuge (Psalm 61:2-3) and the Rock that followed Moses in the wilderness (1 Corinthians 10:4). Of course, Saul becomes Paul and I can't see how Paul relates to a divine name, so I guess I'll have to chalk that one up to the exception that proves the rule.

But you see the pattern emerging. In giving someone a new name, the Lord is acknowledging and activating something of His own nature in them in a very specific way. The fullness of God dwelt in Jesus in bodily form and Jesus now lives in you. So the fullness of God lives in you, but at the same time there is some unique combination of the things of God that fit you specifically. It matches the gifts and commissions placed in you from birth. It shines through every moment you have let Him into.

At the start of this book we thought about how, like a bank note, we carry the hallmarks of value, the image of God and the sliver of glory. But there is something else every bank note needs to be valuable. It needs a unique number to be genuine. That unique number is made up of common digits shared with every other bank note, but the overall combination is unique.

And so with us: the things that happen to us create a unique number in our lives, but as we process the events with Jesus they write a unique name in us, a name that belongs to both of us.

Simon's new name, "Peter" conveys the truth that Peter was a foundation stone in the Church, just as Jesus was its full foundation, and just as His Father was the foundation of everything. The Glory the Father has given to Jesus, Jesus has given to us (John 17:22).

Anointed Gift of God

As I've ministered in the prophetic I've noticed how often the Lord will speak into or about someone's natural name too: its meaning through word play or the origins or reason for their name; through a nickname or by connection to someone else with the same name, sometimes biblical, sometime not.

The phenomenon of nominative determinism shows that what you are called is important. Whatever the source or reason for our natural name, it will have written itself deep into our souls. Our natural names are public, visible, like the head of a nail. But as with a nail, what we can see is only part; there is a whole lot of hidden name driven into core of who we are.

God says to Jerusalem in Isaiah 62 that they will be called by a new name, but to this day Jerusalem is still called Jerusalem. The outer or public name has stayed the same, but there has been a change in the inner and private meaning of the name. "Jerusalem" is a very different idea in the New Testament than it was in the Old.

And so with us. Not everyone has a change to the label they're known by, but I am convinced that the Lord wants to talk with every believer about their name in Him; to reshape its meaning in them.

Jesus hasn't just called me a Jack and a Joker (see the first chapter). In 2007, the year before the Spirit physically shook me up and triggered a major change in who I understood myself to be, Father spoke to me about my name in a way that changed it while leaving it the same too.

To those who had known me for a long time it felt as though I had a totally new name, though in reality it was my original name, just seen differently.

My parents had a Scandinavian friend with a son called "Christen". My mum liked the name and so when I was born she called me "Christen John Forster". But at home I was just "Chris". When I got to school other children would laugh if they discovered my full name or want to know why I had a Scandinavian name with no obvious Norse ancestry. Teachers regularly got my name wrong and for some reason couldn't say my surname either: I was called "Christopher Foster" by more than one teacher at more than one school.

Over the years I would introduce myself simply as "Chris" and I didn't bother correcting any of the variants colleagues might use. But in 2007 I got to know Stephen and Mara Klemich. At some point Stephen picked up that my name wasn't what he thought it was; "Chris" wasn't short for "Christopher". He asked me my full name then looked me in the eye and said, "You should start using it. What does it mean?" Well, my mum had always told me that it was just the Scandinavian form of "Christian", but in my reply I said to Stephen, "It means 'Anointed', so if you put it with my second name 'John' I suppose I'm an 'Anointed Gift of God'."

I was totally surprised by my own response, although I knew where the information had come from. Over the years I had noticed my name didn't upset any computer spell-checkers and so had spotted that while it is pronounced differently, my name was spelt the same as the verb "to christen". At a Christening you anoint the baby's head rather than fully baptise them.

I wasn't totally sure of my translation in the moment, so when I got home I checked it out online. It turned out my assumption was correct, the name "Christen" really does mean "anointed". I took Stephen's words as a prophetic word to me and started to introduce myself and sign off as "Christen".

I still let people call me whatever they like, but I now use my full first name. It might seem a bit arrogant, but actually I am an anointed gift of God and what I have found is that since I started using my full name I have become a lot more confident of this truth. It encourages me to be anointed when I don't feel like it.

The Overcoming Name

Your name is perhaps the most constant thing about you, so your testimony must tell a story about your name. The story around your name is a weapon that defeats the devil (Revelation 12:11). So it shouldn't surprise us that the devil has a deliberate strategy to counterfeit in us the identity Jesus wants to give us.

We get a clue to how he does this in the verse immediately before we read about overcoming the devil by the power of the blood and by our testimony:

"Now the salvation, the power, and the Kingdom of our God, and the authority of His Christ has come; for the accuser of our family has been thrown down, who accuses them before our God day and night." (Revelation 12:10)

The words translated as accuser and accuses in the verse above are the Greek words "kategoros" and "kategoreo" respectively. In English we get the words "Categoriser" and "Categorise" from them.[59]

The devil looks to categorise us. He puts us in a box with a million other people. At the obvious end those boxes might say "sinner", "loser", "bad father" on the lid. These boxes have power over us, because we often carry labels on us that match the labels on the box lid. I sin, so he sticks a label on me that says "sinner"; I fail to get the grades I need so he sticks a label on me that says "loser"; I misunderstand my children's needs so I get the "bad father" post-it note.

But not all the labels on us are necessarily bad or untrue. Some of them can even be words that Jesus has spoken over us, perhaps even the word "overcomer". The problem is, a category is too coarse a way of defining who we are. A category won't let us discover our uniqueness.

As we live life, we will attract labels, but Jesus will never constrain or define us by those labels. Some of the labels will come by hidden manna, but "my words," says Jesus, "will show you truth and that truth will make you free" (John 8:31-32). Sometimes Jesus' words will narrow the path ahead of us, after all we were set free to be "something", not "everything" or "anything", but they will always lead us forward. As a label, even a word given to us by Jesus can lock us into a category instead of letting it drill its way into us to become a part of our secret name.

The first word from Jesus of which I was conscious was the word He spoke to me about being a "Wildcard Joker" or a "Jack of all trades". There have been times when the enemy has used both of these labels to put me in a box.

I felt a great exhilaration when Jesus had first shown me and spoken about my identity in these terms. I found a real liberation in not having to be too serious and focused about my calling; something my striving heart really needed – though I didn't know that at the time.

But at university my need for validation got the better of me and I started to let the idea of these words define me as much as

123

release me. I developed a Joker persona. I wore flamboyant and colourful clothes. I even had a striped pair of trousers with bells at the ankles and braid and ribbons sewn onto the legs. I offset this with a rainbow jumper and a crushed velvet hat with a large gold buckle on it. I wore this ensemble to an exam once. The tinkling bells annoyed my peers no end.

When Jesus had given me the word about being a Joker, He had used a fond image from my childhood. But I had let myself be put into a category with every other clown that ever lived. As I developed a persona based on the category I started making irresponsible choices and almost failed my second year at university as a result.

The "Jack of all trades" category entrapped me more subtly. The proverbial suffix "master of none" locked me into a satisfaction with what was second rate. Eventually Jesus was going to correct my understanding of the label. I was to be a "master of one". But I don't think I misheard Him the first time around. Back then I needed to know I didn't have to be master at something in order to have a go.

The names and words Jesus gives to us work from the inside out. But the categorising devil will take any label he sees on us, even ones given by Jesus, and try to impose an identity on us from the outside.

As the word works in us it respects and works with our uniqueness. Our identity emerges as it grows through the layers of our natural and spiritual DNA and the life history we carry in our soul. A category treats our uniqueness clumsily and restricts our journey and growth.

For Every Child of God

"Bring my sons from afar and my daughters from the ends of the earth. Everyone who is called by my name, that I have created for my glory, that I have formed, yes, that I have prepared." (Isaiah 43:6b-7)

You may or may not have talked to Jesus about your name before, but Father has been preparing you and Jesus is now calling you by it. And I want ask you to take some time to do so here.

Jesus' name, "Yeshua" in Aramaic, was a very common name in His day, but that didn't mean it had no meaning. In fact, the Angel had told both Mary and Joseph that they should name their son "Jesus", which meant "Salvation".

Do you know what your name really means? It's easy to research online if not. Don't just accept the first definition you find, dig a little deeper. You sometimes find a name has come to mean something, but that it originally meant something else. Sometimes a name is linked to a particular person who achieved something memorable. Think about all your names including your surname.

Do you know why your parents gave you the name they did?

I was praying for some people on one occasion and found myself saying to a lady, "You were named after an aunt and you have some of their defining characteristics. But the Lord says not to worry about that because you are not her. You are your own person." The lady immediately told me that she had in fact been named after an aunt and was like her in so many ways, but was fearful because her aunt had become an alcoholic.

There may be good or bad things in the meaning and reasons behind your name, but Jesus wants to put His fingerprints on this label that has penetrated into you, because you have answered to it for years.

Ask Jesus what He has to say about your name and the reasons it was given to you. Also, ask the Lord to add His own mark to your name. I've seen the Lord speak deeply into people through word plays on the syllables of their name, e.g: "You, Val, have Val-ue."

Be honest with the Lord about how you feel about your name. If you're indifferent, ask Him to excite you about it. If you're unhappy He will either need to change your view of your name or He will need to give you a new one. There is no point keeping open a channel for disappointment into your heart.

But even if you see good things hidden in your name, ask the Lord to keep speaking His new name over you, in ways that you can understand but, more importantly, in ways that will change you.

If you are finding it hard to hear or feel anything, try and answer the question that Jesus asked Simon: "Who do you say that I am?"

Tell Jesus who He is to you. Has He redeemed and saved you in practical ways? Is He your Counsellor, your Friend, your Lord etc? It was in seeing Jesus that Simon became Peter.

There was an old married couple who got to see Jesus in the Old Testament. They're not sure if it's an Angel or God Himself (Judges 13:21-22) so the man asks, "What's your name?" He received the reply:

"Why do you ask my name? It is secretly wonderful." (Judges 13:18)[60]

It is part of Jesus' secretly wonderful name that He wants to write into you. So think through all the aspects, titles and names assigned to Jesus in Scripture. There are hundreds of them: He is the Word, the Way, Almighty God, Prince of Peace, Bread of Heaven etc. Let your mind run through all these names and more and see if any stand out to you. Does Jesus want to give one of them to you?

The new name Jesus gives to us is a prophetic word that cuts right into us and runs right through us:

"The word of God is living, and active. Sharper than any two-edged sword and piercing to where soul and spirit divide." (Hebrews 4:12)

Prevailing With God
We are three quarters of the way through this book. My hope is that you have a clearer picture at this point of the story that has made you "you" than you had before you started. This is just information, but it is grist to the mill of transformation. Bring your story before the Lord and be tenacious in asking Him what it all means. Hold

onto to Him like Jacob did, demanding the blessing (Genesis 32:24-30).

Jacob wrestled with God and received the most important name change in Scripture. Jacob became Israel, which means "Prevails with God" – a double-edged name implying that Jacob both won something from God and that he would prevail because God was with him.

I used to wonder why a good God who wants His children to be blessed would need them to wrestle blessing from Him. But I see it now. There are places to go with the Lord that are fantastic, but painful to get to. God's love means He won't take you there if you don't want to go and He needs us to know for ourselves that it was our choice to stay with Him whatever the cost. Which is where we are going to next.

As Christ in us grows we'll find we need to be sure of our choice to keep following. It is God's grace that He sometimes delays telling you who you really are.

But stay persistent. There is a purely personal and private wonder in the name he whispers to you.

Your inner name can only really be known by you and the Lord, because: "...who among men knows the things of a man, except the spirit of the man, which is in him?" (1 Corinthians 2:11)

Endnotes

54. Many ancient manuscripts add the words "to Him" to the phrase "The heavens were opened" in Matthew 3:16. This makes the experience a description of a spiritual state rather than a statement about the weather.
55. Synchronicity, 1952.
56. "Why Susie Sells Seashells by the Seashore: Implicit Egotism and Major Life Decisions", Published in the "Journal of Personality and Social Psychology", 2002.
57. See the chapter "Truly, Newly Human" in The Supra-Natural Life.
58. Macbeth Act 5, Scene 5.
59. Thank you to Carl Wills from whom I got this insight.
60. I prefer to combine the two meanings of the underlying Hebrew word.

CHAPTER 7

A BETTER COUNTRY

"They reached for a better country, a heavenly one. So God is not ashamed to be called their God, in fact He has prepared a city for them." (Hebrews 11:16)

In the heyday of the British Empire, the wealthy of Britain decided to reach for a better country and today, much of what we think of as natural English countryside, was actually designed and built by garden engineers or landscape builders. The most famous garden builder of his day was Lancelot Brown,[61] better known by his nickname, Capability. Capability Brown adopted and adapted an old Greek proverb:

"Civilization happens when old men plant trees under whose shade they shall not sit."

I live in the legacy of a nation built by people who saw their lives within the framework of a bigger picture. The same principle that built Empires holds true in the Kingdom too. But in the Kingdom, the big picture is different and the principle looks very different in practice to the Empire's.

The called life starts with the discovery of who we are as a producer. The first Adam was a gardener but Jesus, the second Adam, was a builder. A producer feeds his family year by year, but a builder leaves a home for the generations that follow him.

The Father's plan for the last phase of Jesus' life was all about legacy and God's big redemptive picture. As Jesus' forebears put it:
"His death shall bring the humble/depraved rest."

It is in our nature to build. As early people spread out from Eden they found a way of making bricks and mortar and proposed a monument, something that would leave their mark in history: "Let's make a city and a tower whose top will reach into heaven; and let us make a name for ourselves." (Genesis 11:4b)

The builders of Babel never finished their tower and the Bible doesn't remember any of their names either.[62] But in the very next chapter of Genesis, God takes hold of a transient shepherd, invites him on a journey and makes him a promise: to give him a land, to make him a nation, to bless him, to make his name great and to bless every family on earth through him (Genesis 12:1-4). There is always a promise implicit in calling.

In his lifetime Abram, or Abraham as he became, only realised one of these promises: he was "blessed". But he was just a blessed nomad with no fixed address. Travelling peoples were looked down on in Abram's time just as they are today. His name wasn't that great.

But today most of the world knows the name of Abraham. Christians, Jews, Muslims and Sikhs all recognise him as a father of their faiths. The other bits of the promise are now demonstrably true too: the strip of land at the crossroads of three continents is still called Israel after Abraham's grandson. His great grandson, Joseph, blessed the whole world with food. And his distant heir, Jesus, has caused more good in the world than any life before or since. Ultimately, everything promised to Abraham found its fulfilment in Jesus.

The builders of Babel, on the other hand, failed to make a name for themselves. They died and that was that. But every promise made to Abraham has been fulfilled in multiple ways since his death, because in life Abraham reached for a promise rather than for a promotion.

We reach for promises by mustard seed sized acts of faith; little things that demonstrate we are waiting for Father to fulfil His word to us. If we've walked with Jesus long enough to have our identity re-shaped then the promise implicit in our calling will now be certain in us, and there comes a time when we need to simplify life and focus on heaven's commitment to us.

For Abraham this meant buying a burial plot in the Promised Land. His death and interment would be a final act of faith in the first promise God ever made to him, that this would be his country. The family grave became an active prophetic legacy to his children's children too (Genesis 49:30-50:26) and around 600 years after God promised Abram the land of Canaan, his family finally settle it.

There is a way of living and even of dying that releases more fruit in our legacy than we saw in our work life. Abraham heads the list of faith heroes in the book of Hebrews. The list ends with the observation that in life, these heroes were:

"...destitute, afflicted and ill-treated, people of whom the world was not worthy..." (Hebrews 11:37d-38a)

The writer goes on to observe that, "...all these, having obtained a testimony through their faith did not receive what was promised, because God had foreseen something better for us, and apart from us they are not complete." (Hebrews 11:38b-39)[63]

In this life there is a testimony to write, but the story only makes sense as part of a bigger story – a story that stretches beyond the ends of our natural span. We are incomplete apart from those who come after us.

Of Whom the World is Not Worthy

Svea was a small lady, less than five feet tall and a singer in Sweden when she and her husband David felt the call of Jesus to become missionaries to Africa. It was 1921 when David and Svea Flood took their son, David Jr, and joined Joel and Bertha Erickson travelling to the Belgian Congo (now the Democratic Republic of Congo) to plant a church.

They travelled into the interior, but were rejected by all the villages they tried to enter. Eventually they cleared a space in the jungle a half-mile outside a village called N'dolera. The village chief wouldn't allow any interaction with his villagers for fear of offending the local gods, but a young boy was allowed to sell chickens and eggs to the Floods and the Ericksons twice a week.

Life was tough in the jungle: constant bouts of sickness, no playmates for Svea and David's son. The Ericksons decided to return to the main missions base over a hundred miles away. The Floods were left on their own. Svea used to talk to the boy who sold them food and tell him Bible stories as best she could. The boy made a childish commitment to Jesus, simply smiling and nodding as Svea explained the gospel to him. Then Svea fell pregnant.

David thought it would be a sign of their convictions to have their baby right where they were and where they believed God had called them to be. But Svea caught malaria and two weeks after giving birth to a daughter, Svea died. Her last words were, "Call her Aina."

Distraught, David buried his wife then took his son and newborn daughter back to the mission base. By the time he arrived there David was seethingly angry with Jesus. He told the Ericksons he was going back to Sweden, but only taking his son with Him. Aina was left at the mission base. Then the Eriksons both died, possibly poisoned by a local chief.

The call of God on the lives of two young couples couldn't have ended with less success: three dead, one bitter and an orphaned little girl. But, "Precious in the sight of the Lord is the death of His godly ones" (Psalm 116:15).

These words are from a Psalm sung at the Passover meal. Jesus sang them on the night that He died (Matthew 26:30) and the words must have meant a lot to Jesus in the hours that followed. But the Psalm refers to "ones" not just to "one". Multiple individuals who, by virtue of Christ in them, fulfil the pattern of Jesus' life by laying it down.

Jesus' greatest victory came in His death. Death, the outcome of mankind's failure, is never a success but it can be, and frequently is, fruitful in the life of the overcomer. For us, "Death is the dropping of the flower, that the fruit may swell."[64]

So baby Aina was adopted by an American missionary couple who renamed her Aggie. At the age of three they took her back to the States.

Aggie grew up and married a man who became the principal of a Christian College in Washington State. The college had a strong Scandinavian heritage and one day Aggie was intrigued to find a Swedish magazine posted anonymously in her mailbox.

She couldn't read the magazine, but flicked through the pages until a photograph caused her to catch her breath. It was a picture of a simple grave marked by a wooden cross with her mother's name on it, "Svea Flood".

She drove to the college to find someone to translate the article. It told the story of a white family who had come to the village of N'dolera; of a baby born to a mother who had died; and of a little boy who had met Jesus through the lady who died.

When that boy grew up he started a school in his village and told the children the stories he had been taught as a child. One by one the children had become Christians. Eventually, most of the village accepted Christ, including the chief who had first banned the missionaries and their God.

The story moved Aggie to track down her real father. She had tried in the past, but to no avail. So when the college offered her husband a sabbatical they made plans to visit Sweden.

They crossed first to London and discovered there was a Pentecostal Missions Convention happening at the Royal Albert Hall. With no knowledge of the programme they just turned up to hear a black preacher talking about the growth of the Church in the Congo. He was the superintendent of a denomination with over 110,000 members.

At the end, Aggie approached him to see if he knew of her mother or father. "Yes," he replied in French through a translator, "Svea led me to Jesus when I was a boy. They had a daughter, but I don't know what happened to her."

Aggie wept and told him her story. "You must come to back to the Congo ... your mother is the most famous person in our history," the preacher told her.

Aggie went on to Stockholm and tracked down her family. Her father was still so bitter with the Lord that he wouldn't allow the name of Jesus to be spoken near him. He was sick in bed, an alcoholic surrounded by old bottles, when Aggie eventually met him.

He cried when he saw Aggie. "I never meant to give you away Aina ... but God forgot us ... it's because of Him."

Aggie told him how his work hadn't been in vain, about the boy who brought them food, the 600 believers in the village they had tried to reach and of the thousands who had came to Jesus through the boy who sold them food. The names of David and Svea Flood were remembered and honoured. By the end of the afternoon David was reconciled with Jesus.

David Flood died shortly afterwards.

Eventually, Aggie was able to visit the Congo. In N'dolera she was greeted by cheering crowds. She met the man hired by her father to carry her as a baby down the mountain and back to the missions base. She knelt and prayed by her mother's grave.

That afternoon the local pastor spoke from John's Gospel and the Psalms.

"I tell you the truth, unless a kernel of wheat falls to the ground and dies, it remains only a single seed." (John 14:24)

"Those who sow with tears will reap with joy." (Psalm 126:5)

Svea obtained a testimony by her life, but without the fruit that came after death she would not have received her promise. Svea, like Jesus, was more fruitful in death than she was in life.

And so it is with the overcomers. They have the blood of the Lamb and the word of their testimony to do battle with, but there is a final part to the verse: "...they did not love their lives even to death." (Revelation 12:11)

This doesn't mean that all overcomers are martyrs, nor that they have to die prematurely. But there is something about their approach to living that is not defined by the life they can hang on to. They know who they are and whose they are. The overcomer doesn't need the trappings of fame or the comforts of success, even if they have them. They are happy just being faithful in reaching for the promises they have received over the years.

The one thing the overcomer does need to do to release a legacy is to endure with Jesus. At the end of the last chapter we thought about how Jacob had to hang on and wrestle a promise out of Jesus, perhaps because Jesus knew what it would cost Jacob to receive it.

There is a tension that everyone who carries a promise from Jesus has to learn to live with if they're going to endure. It's the tension captured in the final verse used as a testimonial to Svea Flood. It is the tension between tears and joy.

It was, "For the joy set before Him that [Jesus] endured the cross, despising its shame." (Hebrew 12:2)

Blessed Are Those Who Mourn

Svea's story moves me to tears almost every time I re-tell it. Eternal life in Christ Jesus is a free gift (Romans 6:23b), but it can cost us everything to follow where it leads us. It cost Svea her health and ultimately her life, but in Svea's mind it was all worth it. She never lost her joy. I can say that because the last words she spoke were, "Call her Aina". In Swedish, "Aina" means "Joy".

The Father doesn't wish pain on us, but Christ in us makes us participators in every aspect of His life, which includes Jesus' persecution.

"If they persecuted me, they will also persecute you." (John 15:20).

There is conflict that comes from the outside, but there is more too. As Jesus grows in us, His compassion and grief over sin replaces our pride and insensitivity towards a sin-broken world. There is a mourning that grows in us as we become like Him.

Either way, for the overcomer who shares Christ's life, the burden is light; it can even be a joy. But for an observer it can seem to be an unbearable offence. The line between joy and offence is a thin one. It is the difference between joy and happiness when put under pressure, which I will need to explain.

But this was the difference between David and Svea. As a couple they both loved Jesus, they loved each other, and they were called together. But as their dream crumbled, David's happiness vanished with it, while Svea's joy looked beyond her own death. In difficult times we find our way through to joy or we let the affront done to us become an offence in us. And, "Blessed is the one who is not offended in Me" (Matthew 11:6).

We're going to explore the nature of joy, but first it helps to understand our pains and struggles a bit differently. We need to see both the privilege and the opportunity in our pain, without buying into the lie that God causes our suffering for our own good.

Filling Up What is Lacking

"Consider it pure joy ... when you come into various types of trial ... And let hopeful endurance have its full work in you, so you are full and complete, lacking nothing." (James 1:2-4)

Paul makes an extraordinary statement just before highlighting the glorious mystery of "Christ in You". If you know Paul's theology the statement can seem to be at odds with Paul's commitment to the complete and sufficient work of the cross. In Colossians, he says:

"Now I rejoice in my sufferings for your sake, so in my flesh I do my share (on behalf of the body which is the church), in filling up what is lacking of Christ's afflictions." (Colossians 1:24)

Paul had joy in his suffering, which is remarkable and is the quality we're aiming for, but the surprise here is in the second half of the verse. Some Bibles translate this phrase as "what is lacking in Christ's afflictions". But the lack is not in the cross, the lack is in Paul.

Paul saw his suffering, his imprisonments, his beatings, his ridiculing, as the fruit of the Word growing in him; as the reworking of Christ's life in Him and as a chance to understand Jesus more deeply.

It was a joy for Paul to experience what Christ experienced, whether glorious or painful, because we can only really "know" someone to the extent that we share similar experiences with them. And Paul looked forward to the day when he would fully know Jesus in experience, just as he was fully known by Him (1 Corinthians 13:12).

Sympathy for someone's misfortune only requires that we are smart enough to know that their pain hurts them. But empathy feels the life of another with them, finding connection and understanding in our common experiences with them. Jesus didn't just sympathise with humanity's plight from Heaven. As the Son of Man He found common ground with us. He became an intermediary with the Father; a High Priest who could feel with us.

But love is supposed to be a two-way street. So when Jesus' life reproduces His experiences in us, whether they are glorious or painful, they give us the opportunity to know Him better and to love Him deeper.

It is not that Christ's life in us is deliberately painful for our sake and it's certainly possible to know salvation without too much discomfort, but if we are determined to keep following His call, we will meet persecution, rejection and anger. Closer to home we will feel that pain of injustice, betrayal, jealousy and competition far more acutely.

Life gives us a fragile heart with a hard shell, while the heart of Jesus is strong but stays soft and open. None of us could cope with full exposure to the suffering caused by sin in our good Father God, who notices every sparrow that falls to the ground. But Christ in us feels like God feels, so it becomes harder to be unmoved in a sin-broken world. Not with judgment and self-righteousness, but with real compassion, grief and grateful humility.

The abundant life Jesus calls us to is a life with the colour contrast turned up. The darkness is darker, but the colours are richer and the light more glorious too.

So to keep walking in our calling we need to find a way of turning both Christ's glory and His suffering into increased intimacy with Him. If we don't find greater intimacy, then our glory will produce pride when it's the humble who inherit the Earth; our sorrows will produce offence, but it's those who mourn who are comforted.

With the right attitude:

"Our momentary light affliction works in us an eternal weight of glory that is beyond compare." (2 Corinthians 4:17)

Pleasure, Happiness, Joy

I said earlier in this chapter that perhaps the difference between joy and offence was as thin as the difference between joy and happiness, just put under the pressure of some pain and disappointment.

We're all made to be producer-maker-builders, but the kind of producer-maker-builder each of us will be is very much shaped by the specific combination of desires and motivations in us, as they work themselves out in the opportunities that come our way. Our unique combination of urges and desires help define us; they are the reason we write the story that becomes our unique name.

We draw energy and wellbeing from the satisfaction of these defining desires, written into every level of who we are; into our bodies, into our souls and into our spirits.

When the body and its senses are satisfied we call it "pleasure"; when the hopes and dreams of the soul are satisfied we call it "happiness"; and when the longings of the human spirit are satisfied we call it "joy". Pleasure, happiness and joy are all connected. Each is the satisfaction of a desire or urge in us. But the desire being satisfied in each case exists in different parts or at different levels of who we are.

Pleasure satisfies my senses. A great meal thrills my senses of taste and smell; music fills my hearing; a sunset my seeing; and physical intimacy my sense of touch. At a deeper level, listening to a story or doing a crossword puzzle satisfies my brain's basic need to see order and solve problems.

But satisfying the needs of the body does not automatically meet the needs of the soul. In fact, it's normally recognised that simply pursuing a life of pleasure is very unsatisfying emotionally.

Pleasure has its place in creating happiness, but its effects are limited; experiencing pleasure can give us emotional energy but not emotional satisfaction. Of course, that emotional energy can be used to push for the things that do satisfy the soul and make us happy: things like raising a family, creating a home or achieving a goal. Pleasure plays a part in happiness, but it is different from it and sometimes it's in conflict with it too.

Pursuing the things that will make us happy normally leaves less room and resource for the things that give us pleasure. Children leave no time for a lie-in, decorating the home costs social time and meals out. But the pleasures we can still fit in become icing on a cake that has the substance needed to satisfy the soul. If you just try eating the cake-icing, it will make you sick well before it sates your hunger (Proverbs 25:16). But without icing the cake could get boring. Without some pleasure we are likely to abandon reaching for the dreams that might have satisfied our soul in the longer term.

Now, I want you to notice that the flow down is greater and feels more natural than the flow up. If you are happy you will find a lot more things pleasurable than if you are sad. Simple food tastes fantastic; five minutes of quiet is like a sauna and a massage. A happy life finds pleasure in its spare moments in a way the pleasurable life doesn't find happiness in all its wide open spaces and freedoms. There is a flow of satisfaction downward from happiness to pleasure, but the flow upwards is more complicated and limited.

I live by the River Thames. Its natural flow is west to east, but daily tides can push a floating object backwards for a while, east to west. But debris will always find its way to the sea. I want you to see clearly the priority of the flow of satisfaction, from the inner person to the outer person, because while most people see the difference between happiness and pleasure, it is surprising how people don't see the difference between joy and happiness.

The relationship and the difference between joy and happiness is very similar to the relationship and difference between happiness and pleasure.

There is a happiness, a satisfaction of the soul, that comes by walking in our calling. But at the beginning of this book we saw that there is a hope beyond calling, and as we've progressed we've seen that this hope is linked to "the rich value of the glory of His inheritance" in you; the unique identity of "Christ in you, the hope of glory". Joy is the satisfaction of our spiritual desires. There is a joy, a satisfaction of the human spirit, that comes by resting in the identity, shape and purpose of Christ in you. Paul found joy even in the frustrations and pains of his calling because he let the frustration that would rob his happiness grow his intimacy with Jesus instead.

Just as pleasure can sometimes be in conflict with happiness, so happiness can be in conflict with joy. God gave Adam a garden and called him to look after it. But when God came looking for Adam, Adam hid in the trees and covered himself with their greenery. Adam's calling provided a barrier to intimacy with God. And intimacy with God is the foundation of joy.

There are levels of joy in every human life, because the Spirit is at work everywhere, wooing and shaping human spirits even while they fight against His activity. And so, as with happiness and pleasure, there is a clear flow downwards from joy to happiness and pleasure. Svea could be happy in the jungle because it trickled down from the satisfaction in her rested spirit. David was happy in the jungle while it satisfied his need to be a producer-maker-builder.

Joy and happiness get confused and rolled into a single experience, which can eventually become a problem. Just as things that once gave us pleasure stop pleasing the unhappy soul, so the things that made us happy can become bitter to the joyless spirit.

Joy, on the other, hand flows down and out. It can find pleasure and happiness sharing a dry sandwich with someone. It is joy, not happiness, that sustains the righteous life – the life that has found rest in its intimacy with Jesus, correctly aligned and positioned as an heir under heaven. But the flow downwards means the righteous life can be exceedingly and outrageously happy too.

When satisfaction flows from the spirit, through the soul and into the senses the Bible calls it "Shalom", a word that means our total wellbeing, body, soul and spirit. We use the word "peace" in our English Bibles. Kingdom life is the interplay of "righteousness, peace and joy in the Holy Spirit" (Romans 14:17): "Righteousness", the alignment and connection we have with heaven; "Joy", the satisfied response of our spirit to that connection and alignment;

and "Peace", the outworking of that "joy" in body and soul.

With joy we can demonstrate a peace from God, a satisfaction of the whole person that surpasses and even defies logical understanding. We can know a different flavour of happiness in the sourest of personal tragedies; a different kind of pleasure in the toughest of awful circumstances.

So we hit another of those spiritual paradoxes: holding on too tight to the things that give us happiness can leave us sad. We have to be able to let things die for the sake of joy.

"Whoever desires to save his life will lose it, and whoever will lose his life for my sake will find it." (Matthew 16:25)

But the amazing thing is, whatever we give up for the Lord He recompenses us for – both in this life and the next (Luke 18:29-30).

The God of Abraham, Isaac and Jacob

In 1787, a young William Wilberforce wrote in his journal that he felt God had given him "two great objects" for his life. The first he is famous for throughout the world, it was to abolish the slave trade. The second is not so well known, but it reflected William's faith too. It was to raise moral standards in the United Kingdom.

Wilberforce died at the end of July 1833, just two weeks before the British parliament finally passed the law outlawing slavery in all of its colonies and dependencies. He had heard just three days before his death that the numbers stacked up and that the bill would pass. But in human terms, under the sun, Wilberforce never received his promise.

Under heaven things are very different. God calls Himself the God of Abraham, Isaac and Jacob and, as Jesus pointed out, He is a God of the living not the dead (Matthew 22:32). So Wilberforce has received his first promise for God, because he is alive in Christ. But, of course, he had a second great object from the Father too, to raise the morals of the nation. Though history forgets it, Wilberforce campaigned on this issue to the same degree as he did slavery. But on the whole he encountered indifference and even scorn from other Christians.

It was the generation of Evangelical social reformers that were to follow him in the Victorian era that acknowledged how Wilberforce inspired and carved out a path for them.

With the abolition of slavery and a growing evangelical engagement in social problems the British Empire reached its zenith in the generation that followed Wilberforce. Wilberforce was a man who reached for a better country. He did so by a faith that sowed his life into two promises. He saw partial results on both fronts in life, but in Christ he has received both promises in full as part of the great cloud of witnesses who cheer on the faithful living. Wilberforce's life and testimony had become the word of God in his generation. The seed that,

"...if it dies, it bears much fruit." (John 12:24b)

Those who walk well in their calling to the ends of their lives produce a greater testimony in their legacy than they do in their moments under the sun. I'm sure of it. I see it in the Bible. I see it in history and I've seen it in practice too. In fact, I had just started writing this chapter when I was reminded of a situation I had the privilege of being close to.

Man is Born For Trouble as the Sparks Fly Upwards

Two days ago a friend, Graham, asked me out of the blue if I'd heard of an author called T. Austin Sparks. I had. In fact, as a four-year old, Mr Sparks had laid hands on me and prayed for me. Just before he died in 1971 Austin Sparks had asked to see my father. He prayed for him too and passed on his sense of commission to my dad.

Austin Sparks was a man whose understanding of the Gospel, the Church and the Kingdom were well ahead of their time. In the 1950's and 60's his insights took him all over the world. He impacted movements and church planters on every continent. In particular, in China he mentored Watchman Nee and the Little Flock movement.

Austin Sparks or TAS as he's sometimes called, believed in the deepening work of the cross in the life and experience of the believer. This was the foundational experience of the overcomers. He also saw church as a living, organic, transformational, missions-sending body and as a training and discipleship centre.

He started a newssheet devoted to these ideas. "Witness and Testimony" went all over the world. And together with a friend TAS built the Honor Oak Christian Centre to embody his vision – a building to house a local church that served the worldwide Church through literature, missionaries, training and conferences. The Centre had meeting rooms, offices and even a printing press.

Eventually, some of the co-leaders he appointed decided they didn't share his vision for a resource church. They wanted to focus on local church. They started to resist his initiatives and his leadership wasn't received. So, with a broken heart, T Austin Sparks resigned from the leadership of the church he'd planted. He stayed with the church, but was now seen as a "difficult member". He was grieving inside for the death of the vision he had carried and which had shaped him as much as he had shaped it; of a vision he believed was God given.

When my parents arrived at the Honor Oak Christian Centre in late 1969, Mr Sparks found a new spark of enthusiasm. He asked for my dad to be made an elder of the church he had once led. Privately, he commissioned my father and then he died.

Three years later my parents and 12 others left the Centre amicably to start a new church. In just over a decade, the Ichthus Christian Fellowship grew to two and half thousand people in multiple congregations. It had over 100 missionaries and a training centre that people came to from all over the world to attend.

The Ichthus Christian Fellowship had become what T. Austin Sparks had started the Honor Oak Christian Centre to be. Over the same period the Centre declined and in the end the building had to be sold. It was bought by Operation Mobilisation and became their new Global HQ. OM use more literature than any other missions agency I know, so the building Austin Sparks had raised the money to develop was still producing literature. It was still being used for missions in line with his dreams.

Theodore Austin Sparks was a good man, and:

"A good man leaves an inheritance to his children's children." (Proverbs 13:22)

In a very real sense, I am a child of one Mr Sparks' spiritual children, my dad Roger Forster. I walk in an inheritance from my spiritual forebears and T. Austin Sparks received his promise in my father. And, I hope, to some degree in me too.[65]

But I'm also deeply challenged to live in a story that is bigger than me. So over the last couple of years I've been sifting through all the things and times I've felt that Father has spoken to me; looking at the patterns and quality of what He's said. There are things that were possibilities for a moment that has now passed. There are things that belonged to me while I served the vision of others. But I'm also noticing the words that seem to be His promises in me of a story that is bigger than me.

I have hopes, dreams and prophetic words that transcend me. They are goals that I can see in life or they could grow out of seeds I can still plant and water. While they are too big to strive after, there are mustard seed actions I can be faithful in taking towards them.

I'm cautious in sharing them, because some things should be kept close to your heart and not bandied around too freely. So I'll just share them in their broadest form, but I want you to prayerfully think about whether you have similar hopes and promises from the Lord, things that could be your legacy.

So I both hope for and believe I have a word from Jesus about being involved in events that lead to revival and social reformation in the UK. And I have a dream about helping people to see Jesus more clearly through Scripture.

There are others, but too personal to share. With all of them I can see there are things I need to do, which may mean not doing other worthy things. But with all of these longer term visions there is a likelihood that I will see Jesus' faithfulness to our relationship beyond the natural span of life.

Paul once expressed his desire to preach the gospel where it hadn't been preached before and not to build on the foundations laid by others. So he told the church in Rome he would visit them but not stay there (Romans 15:20). The gospel had been in Rome for half a generation before Paul got there. But the last few years of Paul's life were dominated by Rome, imprisonment, arrests and finally execution. During this time all Paul could do was write a few letters.

Jesus got hold of some of those letters and got His Church to see them as special. They were included in the Bible and today Paul has preached through them to every new place the Gospel has ever come to. In his letters Paul sowed into a desire and a promise that seemed to be frustrated in the natural.

Setting Your Face Towards Jerusalem

The word Jesus received at His baptism would have told Him that: He would be poured out to death and wounded to bring healing to those whose sin merited the punishment (Isaiah 53). But it was only in the final months of Jesus' ministry that He "set His face towards Jerusalem" (Luke 9:51) and started simplifying His ministry, so that His death would bring rest to the depraved but humble.

As your life story comes together you may find it leads you through places your younger, less joy-filled self, would never have chosen to go; places that strip off the possibilities and require us to give up past pleasures. It is the anticipation of joy that helps us walk through the valleys that cast the deepest shades of death over us. Sometimes in these dark places we're helped by the promises the Lord has given to us; other times it's in these valleys that we see clearly what His promises are.

I don't expect you to get all the answers now, but start dialoguing with Jesus about the eternal promises He's given you. As you need to see them and act on them, you will. I can say that because the phase of calling we're entering into is most obviously about the Lord's faithfulness to you as an heir. You might mess up, but He stays faithful to His promises.

Endnotes

61. Lancelot (Capability) Brown, 1716-1783.

62. Tradition and the Sumerian accounts link Nimrod the city-founding rebel of Genesis 10 to Babel, but the Bible doesn't make this connection.

63. Some might point out that this passage assumes we have all our promises in Jesus and that this style of being completed by our scions is now finished. But this is being too narrow with the text. The passage starts looking for the city prepared by God and that finally comes with Jesus' second coming. So it is safe to see a pattern for walking in faith that applies to all ages. The writer is simply illustrating the principle by the promises the Church now walks in.

64. "Prayers from the Plymouth Pulpit", Henry Ward Beecher, Christian Minister and Social Reformer, 1867.

65. Like Sparks, I'm deeply committed to the work of the cross in the experience of the believer, although I didn't know that this was one of his big themes until I rang my father earlier today to check my own memories and facts.

CHAPTER 8

ETERNITY

"He has made everything beautiful in its time. He has also set eternity in their hearts, without which man would not find out the work which God has done from the beginning to the end." (Ecclesiastes 3:11)

Back in chapter two we noted Sartre's comment that life has no meaning outside of eternity. But every heart is connected to eternity, whether it knows it or not. It is by this heart connection that every twist and turn of life, every pressure and even every contamination of the soul, can find eternal meaning and beauty. Eternity in us gives us the ability to see God's work from start to finish.

We've already seen how, from the beginning, Jesus' ancestors up to Noah revealed the shape of Jesus' earthly life, from eternity, through birth and to death. We've seen how this gives us a framework to understand our own calling by:

"God the producer-maker-builder is appointed a mortal man/ begotten/of sorrow. The glory of God descends to dedicate/a teacher, his death shall bring the humble/depraved rest."

But Noah wasn't Jesus' last forebear and Jesus' line has more to tell us. In fact, the names from Noah's son Shem to Abram tell us something about how Jesus became Christ the Anointed Saviour, the name above all other names, in both this age and the age to come. They take us from eternity past, through life, anointing and resurrection, into eternity to come.

The stories covered in Genesis by the ten generations from Shem to Abram are all about fame and leaving a name behind; a name to be remembered by. Interestingly, Jesus' ancestors speak to the same subject. You see it straight away if you translate the first five names from Shem to Peleg. Using standard Bible dictionaries they read:

"Name / renown / fame / essence (Shem) healer / releaser (Arpachshad)[66] sent (Shelah)[67] from the other side (Eber)[68] the divide / separation (Peleg)[69]".

Tidied up, these names start a sentence:

"The name/essence of the healer/releaser sent from the other side of the divide:"

A heavenly healer/releaser has crossed into this life. What follows is going to tell us what that healer/releaser is famous for; something of the secretly wonderful name He carries.

The next five names are the ones that I mentioned in chapter two, the first names that I noticed which seemed to speak about Jesus by type and quality. They are the names that got me speculating for gold in Jesus' genealogy. I could use standard sources to translate all five and they would work, but I've noticed something deeper in the meanings of the last two names, Terah and Abram, so let me explain them first.

First, "Terah" is actually spelt "Terach" in the Hebrew text of the Old Testament. As a name, most researchers agree that the name means "wanderer" or even a "wild goat". I guess wild goats do wander in the desert, so that would explain that connection. It is quite possible to see the quality of a wanderer in Jesus. After all, He observes that He has nowhere to call home (Luke 9:58).

It has been pointed out that "Terach" is a Pagan name with no obvious connection to a Hebrew word. But to Hebrew ears, the name would have sounded the same as two Hebrew words put together: "t-r" meaning "dove" and "ruach" meaning "wind" or "spirit". So Terach's progeny would have heard his name as "Dove-Spirit", which is a wonderful way of describing the Holy Spirit. But actually, there is a simpler way of hearing the name "Terach" as two Hebrew words. You simply put the letter tav in front of "ruach". When used this way, the letter tav marks out the noun that follows it for special attention. So "Terach" could mean "very spirited" or even something like "marked by the Spirit" or "Spirit-marked", which is a great way of describing the Messiah.

Finally, we come to Abram, a name made up of two Hebrew root words. "Ab" which means "father" and "ram" which means to be "lifted up" or "raised up". So Bible dictionaries translate Abram as "Exalted Father" or "Great Father". Certainly Jesus is called "Eternal Father" in Isaiah, so even though it might seem odd, this translation could be used as a quality of Jesus, as part of His renown.

But there is no reason why the Father should be passive in our translation of "Abram". We could also translate Abram as "Raised up by the Father" and this is something that Jesus is certainly world famous for.

So putting everything together we discover:

"The renown/essence of the releaser sent from the other side of the divide: He's a friend/shepherd,[70] a vine,[71] a lamp,[72] a wanderer/ marked by the Spirit, raised by the Father."

It was the Spirit's job to activate the essence already in Jesus and it was the Father's job to raise Him, both physically and metaphorically. Jesus' body was raised after death, but so was

His renown. We've explored this same pattern in the life of every believer who walks in his or her calling. The Spirit will activate new things in you, lead you and change you. You will be resurrected with Christ and something about your secretly wonderful name will find a memorial in eternity and a legacy in history.

It is in such contrast to the way the founders of Babel looked to leave a legacy. They built a city with mud and straw. It didn't last. But the overcomer has a promise to be raised up and, as we will see, he builds with something more enduring.

"A false testimony will perish, but a person who listens speaks to eternity." (Proverbs 21:28)

An Eternal City

As the last seconds of the last millennium ticked away the world's media turned its eyes towards Sydney in Australia, the first city in the world to pass from 1999 into 2000. Over a billion people watched the Sydney celebrations as they happened. The Harbour Bridge became a moving wave of flame above a smiling face, the orchestra crescendoed as the fireworks reached a climax of fire. Then the music stopped and darkness returned as a single word was written in flame across the Harbour Bridge and church bells rang in the new millennium. The word was "Eternity", written in fifty-foot high copperplate handwriting, a flourish on the "E" and underlined by the tail of the "y".

The moment was recreated that summer at the opening ceremony of the Sydney Olympic Games. This time up to four billion people watched. All over the world people discussed the meaning of "Eternity."

In fact "Eternity" is the single word testimony of a man who has profoundly impacted the soul of the city he grew up in.

Arthur was born in Sydney into a family of alcoholics. The family business was prostitution and the petty crime that went with it. At the age of 12, Arthur was made a ward of the state. He started work at age 14 in a coal mine. Within a year he was in prison for the first of many visits.

By his twenties Arthur had established a business of sorts, moving alcohol between the pubs and brothels in the Surrey Hills area of Sydney. He gambled and broke into houses to feed his habits. Then the First World War happened.

Arthur returned from France with a missing eye, shell-shocked and with permanent physical damage caused by exposure to poison gas. Arthur didn't have far to fall, but fall he did. Slipping into full time alcoholism, with only the funds to buy methylated spirits, Arthur lived on handouts, which is what led him to St Barnabas' Church on August 6th 1930. You had to listen to a talk before you ate and, wanting a better life, Arthur had dropped to his knees to receive Jesus when the appeal came.

Christ in Arthur gave him the strength to stop drinking. As his self-respect grew, Arthur found others respected him more too. Arthur found a regular job. Then some months after meeting Jesus he heard a fiery preacher shout out, "I wish I could shout 'Eternity' through all the streets of Sydney."

Arthur left the building, but later recalled, "His words were ringing through my brain as I left the church. Suddenly I began crying and I felt a powerful call from the Lord to write the word, 'Eternity'." Arthur could hardly write. He could scratch out his name if he needed to. But he had a piece of chalk in his pocket so he bent down and wrote in a beautiful copperplate script two feet wide the single word, "Eternity." He had added a flourish to the "E" and the "y" curled back under the other letters.

For over thirty years Arthur Stace wrote his one-word message on the streets and buildings of Sydney. Newspapers discussed what it meant and who was behind the enigmatic word. Others came forward to claim responsibility, but Arthur stayed anonymous, getting up at 5am, praying for an hour and then walking to wherever he felt the Spirit lead him to write his sermon on the roads and walls.

Arthur's testimony only came to light in 1956 when his pastor saw him writing "Eternity" on a pavement. The minister asked outright, "Are you Mr Eternity?"

"Guilty, your honour," replied Arthur. Then a newspaper interviewed Arthur and his story was out. It had an impact wherever people heard it.

Arthur went on writing "Eternity" on pavements and walls until he died in 1967. In total he had written the word "Eternity" over half a million times. But because he wrote in chalk, only two copies written by him remain; one on a piece of cardboard and one on the inside of a bell.

Like chalk in the rain, "...life ... is a vapour, it appears for a little while and then it is gone." (James 4:14b)

Its substance may go, but a life that has heard heaven can still "speak to eternity" by its testimony. If life seems disappointing, if we miss its natural opportunities, we should always remember we weren't made for history, we were made for eternity. And every time we act on heaven's initiative in this life we draw eternity that bit closer. Heaven comes on earth through lives that build according to the promises of eternity.

Gold, Gems and Pearls

In Revelation at the end of the ages at the fulfilment of history, a city comes down from heaven. It is the new Jerusalem, a city prepared by God as a restful home for mankind with his Maker. This is the better country we are all reaching for by faith. But look closely and you'll see that that city is us, the bride of Christ.

"I saw the holy city, New Jerusalem, coming down out of heaven from God, prepared as a bride adorned for her husband." (Revelation 21:2)

We've answered Jesus' call and we've hung on to Him through the struggles until, like Israel, we receive a promise from Him, a word that pierces into us, changing who we are, a powerful urge to write "Eternity" with the chalk of our lives. That promise is our "better country". It is a heavenly seed of an eternal idea that belongs to us in a way that can never be taken away, because in a real sense the idea is *us*. So Arthur Stace became "Mr Eternity". We become the bricks being built into God's house (1 Peter 2:5a). We are the seed being sown into God's field. We are the lives prepared for union with Christ.

As a producer, Father gave Adam a garden; it made sense of his essence and his commission. But a river flowed out of Eden and as people spread out into the world, in line with their commission to fill the earth, they would have discovered raw materials in those waters; materials that once mastered could have made them builders of an eternal city: gold, precious stones and something called "bdolach" (Genesis 2:12).

Now "bdolach" probably refers to freshwater pearls,[73] although most Bibles say "bdellium", which is a plant, or they say "aromatic resin" or "gum" which you can get from the bdellium plant. There are technical reasons why "bdolach" is better translated "pearls" (see the endnotes). But quite apart from these, freshwater pearls are a feature of flowing water in temperate climates, so pearls can be found with gold and gem stones in rivers in Mesopotamia; and as fresh water pearls, something interesting becomes apparent: there is a connection between the raw resources of Genesis and the finished work of Revelation. We can see the beginning and the end of God's work.

Gold, gems and pearls are the materials that the New Jerusalem is built from.[74] The walls and streets are pure gold, inset with every kind of precious stone and the gates are pearly (Revelation 21:18-21). These are the materials that God has always intended to be used for building[75] and it seems that God has found them in us. In Hebrew, Adam's name can mean "earth" and it's interesting that the gold, gems and pearls are found where the river, symbolic of the spiritual life, runs through our earthy humanity.

153

There is gold in us. God put a deposit of glory in us. If you're looking for gold you look at the bends and turns in the river;[76] the defining moments of our stories; the points where God's plan or man's rebellion caused life to take an unexpected turn. That's where the gold collects, but so does a lot of silt, so you sift for gold, filtering and washing it out of the mud.

There are gems in us. Gems stones are ordinary earth that has been put under such extreme pressure that it takes on a new crystalline form; beauty from ashes. But to see the crystals you often have to crack open a few rocks.

And there are pearls too. The precious droplets of victory made by the layers of grace that subsume the rubbish that has gotten into us. You have to dive deep for the pearls.

The adornments and the substance of the New Jerusalem are the beauty and worth of our life story in Christ.

When we die we lose everything earthy in us, but we do take two things from this life into the next. First, we take our relationships (Luke 19:9); second, we take our stories. But seeing as everyone we know is known by their story, it is not surprising that what is really eternal about us is the story.

Over a seven-year period every atom in your body will have been replaced, but you will still be you, because your story ties every configuration of atoms that will ever make up your body into a whole and unique person. And there is glory in your story, the gold, the gems and the pearls are all there in your testimony. The victories of the cross in every bend, pressure and piece of grit in the river of life.

The Kingdom of God, says Jesus, is like "treasure" (gold and gems) "hidden in a field"; it is like a "precious pearl" at a market (Matthew 13:44-46). In Jesus' parable someone gives up everything to get the gold, gems and pearl, but while we are often taught that we need to give up everything to gain the Kingdom, Jesus doesn't actually say that. In Jesus' parable the Father could be the merchant or treasure seeker as equally as it could be us. It is that mysterious entanglement again. Is it you or is it the Lord?

We shouldn't forget that the Father gave up His beloved Son and the Son gave up His life to acquire us.

But it is interesting to note that these eternal materials were not found in the Garden of Eden. They were only available as mankind walked in the commission to fill up and subdue the whole earth. The testimony that speaks to eternity is written by walking in commission.

Little Things Towards the Big Picture

"He made known to us the mystery of His will ... with a view towards a suitable stewardship for the fullness of the times, that is, the summing up of all things in Christ..." (Ephesians 1:9-10a)

The "summing up of all things in Christ" is the end towards which history flows because, "All things have been created through Him, *and for Him*" (Colossians 1:16b).

Christ in us puts His feet down on every dark corner of the world, through missionaries, yes, but also through painters and decorators, taxi drivers and plumbers, even through graffiti artists with just a piece of chalk.

One of the things that most moves me about Arthur Stace's story is that the thing the Lord asked him to do was so simple and yet he did it. In doing it, all of the rubbish of Arthur's childhood became a beautiful counterpoint to the commission of his later life. But more than that, his obedience has drawn the history of a whole city into the story of how all things are summed up in Christ.

Sometimes I think we miss our destiny because, like Naaman, we can't see the point in the simple thing we've been asked to do (2 Kings 5:10-11).

Today you will find that one word sermon "Eternity", written in Arthur's style, not in chalk but in aluminium and set permanently in the paving of Sydney Square. Australia's National Museum has an "Eternity" gallery; and the city council has had to trademark the word to stop it being commercially abused. Arthur has inspired poets, writers, artists, academics and city planners.

In the New Jerusalem I fully expect to find "Eternity" written in the gold, gems and pearls of Arthur's life.

So listen and be faithful to what you've heard and:

"Do not be ashamed of the testimony of our Lord ... but join with me in suffering for the gospel according to the power of God, who saved us and called us with a holy calling ... which was granted us in Christ Jesus from all eternity." (2 Timothy 1:9)

And your testimony can speak to eternity, even if your name gets forgotten in this life.

In Arthur Stace, Jesus became a renowned graffiti artist. The Spirit activated an idea in Arthur and he performed for an audience of one, his heavenly Father. And that Father has raised him up, both physically and by reputation.

Hold On to The Promise

I want to finish our journey into your story by thinking one last time about promise. Arthur Stace had it, Svea Flood had it, T. Austin Sparks had it, and so have countless others whose names we don't know, but will one day learn in eternity.

Sometimes we see the effects of someone's promise, even though we don't know their names. For instance, I mentioned the mini-revival we had at Royal Holloway College when I was a student. It all started in the first week of my second year at university, when the Spirit fell on a meeting we were holding in a small Methodist hall a stone's throw from campus. One person got delivered and lots more were filled with the Holy Spirit and spoke in tongues for the first time.

Now, years later, after we had planted a church to reach onto the same campus, a student heard me mention Pentecostal pioneer Smith Wigglesworth. The name rang a bell for her and she explained that her great grandfather had known Smith Wigglesworth. In fact, he lived in Englefield Green and had gone to the Methodist church, the same one in which the Spirit had fallen on us as students in the mid 1980s. We did a bit of research and it turned out that her great grandfather had been saved in the Azusa Street Revival in California in 1906. It also seemed that Smith had come and spoken at the Methodist church.

Everything made sense to me. The Methodist Hall had always felt more open than the other buildings we used. I don't believe in magic places per se, but I do believe that God keeps the promises he makes to people in places, even when they've shuffled off this mortal coil to join the chorus of the choir invisible. Now Smith Wigglesworth may or may not have spoken at Englefield Green Methodist Church, but what I am sure of is that there were people in the church who had prayed for the Spirit to fall and who had asked the Lord to use the building, perhaps even to reach the students on the campus they could see from their front door. In response, God had a made a promise to them, which He fulfilled in us, way after those original dreamers had gone on to glory.

Father is far more faithful to His promises than we are. If He gives you a promise you can be sure it will change the world eventually! So the enemy will try to stop you getting to the point in your walk with Jesus where His word to you becomes a promise in you. His tactics haven't changed since the beginning.

In Genesis chapter one we had an eagle-eye view of man's creation; in the next two chapters we get down in the dirt with Adam and Eve.

These two chapters are a beautifully constructed narrative. In their original form they were a single unit made up of seven scenes or sections, all balanced around the middle scene, verses six to eight of chapter three, where the man and the woman eat the fruit and their experience of the world changes for the worse.

One of the key features of the whole passage is the occurrence of the phrase "LORD God". In Hebrew, the covenant name of God, "YHWH", is joined to the general word for God, "Elohim". The joining of these two names appears more times in this block of scripture than it does in the rest of the Bible[77] put together. In fact, the name "YHWH" is lost to mankind after these events in the Garden until it is revealed again to Moses (Exodus 6:3).

So the use of "LORD God" in this passage is telling us something important. It tells us that in humanity's innocence, the transcendent Creator God of Genesis was also the intimate and immanent relational YHWH of Covenant. The "Lord God" is "YHWH-God-who-is-known-by-His-promises".

As Scripture progresses, God will re-attach lost revelations about His character to the name "YHWH": "I am YHWH who promises to heal you" (Exodus 15:26); "I am YHWH who promises to make you holy" (Leviticus 20:8), etc.

The only section of Genesis chapters two and three in which God is just called "Elohim" (the powerful but distant God of creation), is in the conversation between the woman, the snake and the man (who is present the whole time, but silent throughout).

"Now the snake was craftier than any animal of the field which **YHWH-God-who-is known-by-His-promises**[78] had made. He said to the woman, 'Has **God** really said, "You shan't eat from any tree in the garden?"' The woman said to the snake, 'We can eat the fruit of the trees of the garden, but the fruit of the tree which is in the middle of the garden, **God** has said, "You shan't eat of it, neither shall you touch it, lest you die."' The serpent said to the woman, 'You won't actually die, for **God** knows that in the day you do eat it, your eyes will be opened, and you will be like **God**, knowing good and evil.'" (Genesis 3:1-3)

In order to disconnect the man and woman from their identity, the serpent first separates them from the intimacy and promises of YHWH-God-who-is-known-by-His-promises. The serpent focuses them on the more abstract "Elohim" or "God". "God" is a concept, it is not a proper name. It is an office to hold, a function to perform. The word "God" is an empty canvas onto which you can paint any picture you like. Which is, of course, what the snake is going to do. His craftiness leads the woman into the mistake of replying to the snake on his terms, referring simply to "God" rather than to "YHWH-God-who-is-known-by-His-promises". So the conversation progresses and the rest is history.

The devil can attach any meaning he likes to the label "God" and so, in his final words, the snake sows seeds of doubt regarding the truthfulness and goodness of God. He paints in Adam and Eve's minds his version of what God's character is like. God is controlling and hoards power. He then invites mankind to become like the image of the god he has painted; to take on this image by doing something to achieve it.

By eating the fruit together the man and the woman fix a distorted image of God into their souls. They disconnect themselves from the true image, along with all YHWH's promises to them.

There is no real creativity or freedom outside of the Spirit of God and so the devil's tactics and strategies have remained pretty much unchanged over the millennia.

He looks to make God feel remote and distant; transcendent but not immanent; full of power but not known by His promises. In the absence of intimacy and promise He paints a picture of God in his image and sets us striving after it to achieve the value we already have.

Perhaps that is why seeing Jesus is involved in our transformation, our identity and our value.

"But we all, with unveiled face see as in a mirror the glory of the Lord, are transformed into the same image from glory to glory..." (2 Corinthians 3:18)

Because, "...however many are the promises of God, in Him is the 'Yes.' And through him is the 'Amen,' to the glory of God through us." (2 Corinthians 1:20)

Jesus is the full revelation of the God-who-is-known-by-His-promises.

There are around 1,000 names and titles of God and/or Jesus in the Bible, yet I am constantly amazed at how many people only refer to God as "God". So before we finish I want to suggest an exercise to you. As a younger man I was challenged to put the basic YHWH names of God into what we call the Lord's Prayer. After the phrase, "Hallowed be your name" or "Your name be honoured", depending on how you learnt it, I would put in one of the YHWH promise names of God and I would then think of how God had been that promise to me in the past. Then I would thank Him for it.

Which is why it's so useful to know your own story.

When I was first diagnosed with cancer I remember going home from hospital at weekends and crying with fear and anger in my bed. I challenged the Lord as to "why"? Someone suggested I read Job. I tried, but at the time I didn't really get the book. I did get the concept, however, and I became aware that I was finding peace inside. I knew God as "YHWH Shalom", God-who-promises-peace, well before I knew Him as "YHWH Rophe", God-who-promises-to-heal-you.

So my challenge is for you to take on a similar exercise. Get to know God by His faithfulness to His promises – promises that you will find the "Yes" and "Amen" to in Jesus. If you can't see the promise fulfilled in your testimony just yet, claim it in Jesus anyway.

As you get comfortable with His generic promises, be deliberate in asking for something personal, for a hidden name that becomes you.

Seeing Jesus in God's names is a spiritual exercise. I can't guarantee it will open up your revelation for you, but it is the kind of exercise the Lord can use and He wants you to share His secretly wonderful name with you. So I do pray it opens up revelation for you.

Conclusion

I have no idea where you are on your journey with Jesus; whether you're just starting out and are learning to be faithful with what you have naturally; or whether you've run ahead into the future before you've learnt all you could have and now need to return to a past call. Certainly you'll have noticed that in this last section I've used other people's testimonies more than I've used my own. That's because I have less experience in this phase of life than the previous stages. But nothing I've taught is simply theory. It is all grounded in experience as well as the Bible.

Perhaps that is why I am so keen that the Christian life is an experience. In every other subject I'm happy reading theory, but with Jesus it has to be real as well as true. To be honest, I wouldn't believe half the theory if I hadn't seen it work in practice. Life is a story that has to be lived, not just read and thought about.

You can't be an overcomer without things to overcome and you can't have a story without a mission, conflict and struggle before the reward and rest. To know glory means to know pain as well; and to really find your life means losing it first.

But it is all worthwhile for the glorious and mysterious truth of Christ in you. It is why Paul can write: "For to me to live is Christ, and to die is even more so" (Philippians 1:21).

One day, Habakkuk tells us, "The Earth will be filled with the knowledge of the Glory of YHWH as the waters cover the sea" (Habakkuk 2:14). If you read the surrounding verses you discover that the world is not an easy place; it is full of evil; but in this context the glory of Christ in you will be unmissable.

So press on for the prize of the upward call of God (Philippians 3:14) and write a testimony in the blood of the Lamb that will echo in eternity. I'll leave you with some encouragement on your adventure from Sam Gamgee, as he put it in the film version of "The Lord of the Rings":

"It's like in the great stories, Mr Frodo, the ones that really mattered. Full of darkness and danger they were, and sometimes you didn't want to know the end because how could the end be happy? How could the world go back to the way it was when so much bad had happened? But in the end it's only a passing thing this shadow, even darkness must pass. A new day will come, and when the sun shines it'll shine out the clearer. Those were the stories that stayed with you, that meant something even if you were too small to understand why. But I think Mr Frodo, I do understand, I know now folk in those stories had lots of chances of turning back, only they didn't. They kept going because they were holding on to something."

There's a glorious life ahead of you. Not an easy life, but certainly a joy-filled one. You can keep going and you will not turn back because you're holding onto Jesus and He is faithful.

In this book we've thought about your story in three phases: the things we need to do to be faithful with what we have; the identity Father gives us; and the fruit He wants to receive in us. Going forward, you can think of these three phases as captured by a simple question to be answered in prayer.

- Calling: What should I be doing now?
- Identity: Who does Jesus say I am?
- Value: What are the promises I carry for creation?

You can discover God's plan and promises for you, and in their discovery you'll feel His attention and know your value.

So, "...that those who have been called may receive the promise of the eternal inheritance" (Hebrews 9:15b).

Endnotes

66. Josephus linked the "Arpachshad" with the "Chasad" or "Kassadim", the people who came from Chaldea, and so some sources link the name to the region. But this is putting the cart before the horse. The people in this section of the Bible gave their names to regions, they didn't take them from them. Hitchcocks Bible Dictionary links the name to an old Arabian word meaning "healer" or "releaser".

67. "Shelah" can mean "sent" or "thrown away". There is another Shelah in the Bible, but his name is spelt differently in Hebrew.

68. "Eber" can mean "to pass through", but the BDB Theological Dictionary translates Eber as "One From Beyond", or "From The Other Side". The name "Eber" is a part of the word "Hebrew".

69. "Peleg" means a "division/divide" or "separation/separate". The word can be used for a canal or trench.

70. "Reu": Most likely means "friend" or "shepherd" from a root that means "pasture". Jesus is the friend who dies for us (John 15:3); the shepherd who lays down his life for his sheep (John 10:11).

71. "Serug" is a thin twisting "branch" or a "vine". Jesus is the vine we are grafted into (John 15:4-5).

72. "Nahor": The root can mean either something bright or something flowing, so "Nahor" can be a "lamp" or it can mean "snoring" or "snorting". Put the two ideas together and it also means "anger". You would hope that Nahor's parents chose a positive name though, so we will assume his name means "a lamp" or "a light". Jesus is the light come into the world (John 12:46)

73. Most translations of the Bible follow the King James Version, which assumed the word was meant to be "bdellium" and link it to a plant that produces an aromatic resin. But "bdolach" is described in Numbers 11 as being like coriander seeds, which do look like small pearls. The Moffat Bible translates "bdolach" as pearls.

74. Interestingly, we are also told that the rebellious city of Babylon had also collected and adorned or gilded itself in these same three elements (Revelation 18:16). In Babylon the façade was gold, gems and pearls; in Jerusalem these are the substance.

75. Note that Paul writes to the church in Corinth encouraging them to metaphorically build on the foundation laid by Christ with gold and precious stones rather than with hay and straw (1 Corinthians 3:12).

76. I want to credit Stephen Klemich for the metaphorical observation that both gold and silt collect where a river changes directon.

77. "LORD God" appears 20 times in Genesis 2-3 and a further 16 times in the rest of Scripture.

78. I have expanded the words used for God in my version of these verses to bring out the subtleties of their use.

ABOUT THE AUTHOR

Growing up in the Ichthus Christian Fellowship as the son of Roger and Faith Forster, Christen is a second-generation leader, pastor and teacher. He has planted churches, mobilised youth teams, led congregations and served in mission contexts in the UK and overseas. In 2010 Christen founded the *Supranatural Life* ministry as part of a vision to help the UK Church step into a more pervasive, intense and  intimate experience of the presence of God.

Christen is married to Judith and they have three teenage children. In his spare time Christen reads, plays bridge, cycles, enjoys theatre and film and spending time with his family. Visit his website at: **www.supranatural-life.com**

THE SUPRA-NATURAL LIFE

Jesus said He had come to give us an abundant life. This promise is like the open sky above us, but it is only as we dare to fly higher with Him that we begin to see the possibilities beyond our old horizons. What does this "abundant life" look like?

- It is an adventure-filled challenge
- It is a life lived in connection with Heaven by the Holy Spirit
- It is a journey into the fullness of God's favour, supernatural encounters and spiritual authority
- It is a life naturally connected to meaning and purpose

This book is the first in a series designed to guide the reader into a more Spirit-led and Heaven-conscious life. It is aimed at those who long for a deeper spiritual experience, but struggle with how to step into it. These books capture and pass on the lessons the author has learned that have radically changed his own expectations of life and

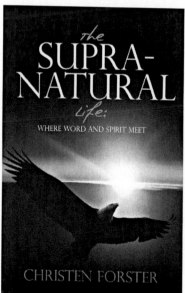

ministry. In them he addresses the misunderstandings and pitfalls that commonly hinder us from becoming all we were made to be.

"Christen openly and humbly demonstrates that this is a journey wrought with challenges ... But there is no greater adventure!" – LYNN GREEN, International Director, YWAM